I AM KING PART 1:

An Unveiling Story from South Louisiana.

Joshua D. Jackson

Copyright © 2019 by Joshua D. Jackson All rights reserved. This book or any portion thereof may not be reproduced or used in any manner whatsoever without the express written permission of the publisher except for the use of brief quotations in a book review.

Printed in the United States of America

First Printing

ISBN 978-1-943284-59-7 (pbk.)

ISBN 978-1-943284-58-0 (ebk)

A2Z Books Publishing Lithonia, GA 30058

www.A2ZBooksPublishing.net

Manufactured in the United States of America

A2Z Books Publishing has allowed this work to remain exactly as the author intended, verbatim.

CONTENTS

Chapter 1: The Beginning 1

Chapter 2: Baby Joshua 13

Chapter 3: The Developing of a Growing Boy 23

Chapter 4: The Painful Challenges 31

Chapter 5: Product of My Environment 41

Chapter 6: Life Changing Legal Challenges 59

Chapter 7: A Child Traumatized 72

Chapter 8: The Adoption 92

Chapter 9: The Lessons Learned While Growing 103

Chapter 10: New Family 117

Chapter 11: From A Boy To A Man 130

Sneak Peak: I Am King Part 2 146

CHAPTER 1

THE BEGINNING

«Life isn't about finding yourself. Life is about creating yourself...
So let's BEGIN!»
--George Bernard Shaw

Linda Lucky and Jasper Jackson were two children out of Independence, Louisiana, a small town about forty-five minutes from New Orleans. They'd known each other from childhood because of their parents. Mildred Smith was the mother of Jasper and Helen Lucky was Linda's mother, both were longtime co-workers at the Oyster House in Amite, Louisiana.

When Linda and Jasper came of age, they started to work there as well, shucking oysters until their hands grew blisters from opening the shells with knives. Jasper had been a field worker with his grandfather since a kid, so hard work was nothing to him at all. He didn't see his father much; Charlie Jackson, who was on the road a lot singing and chasing women as if he wasn't married to Mildred. A talented man none the least but, was just never there for his children.

Jasper had four other siblings, some were skilled workers, preachers, and others just joined the service with their uncles and became veterans. Mildred taught all of them humility, compassion, and that showing love throughout their family was important in God's eyes. Their great Grandfather taught them how to be great self-employed workers, entrepreneurs, and strong-willed individuals! This would later show to be true in each one of their future endeavors.

Linda, on the other hand, was in a total opposite situation. This is a girl that grew up being spoiled by her grandmother and her father as I personally feel all girls should be. She was a very private individual so; I had to do some digging to get as much information as I could so just stay with me. Linda was the oldest out of all five siblings and she played a type of mother role as well.

Her mother's relationship with her was controversial. It was mysterious, hateful, jealousy, envy, and weird altogether. Let's take for instance, Helen not liking the father/daughter relationship between Linda and her husband. There are stories that it was a bond that couldn't be broken between the two. Now, he was a father that stepped out on Helen quite a bit which may have caused her to be hateful but, I've heard from her relatives that she's been that way.

As for Linda, she got her way with her father. So, as a result, Helen would treat Linda like an unwanted stepchild! It got so bad between them that Linda, although being one with hurtful secrets, came out and said that Helen would give her birth control pills at 9-10 years old!

Back in those days, it was said to be one of the ways to stop a girl from having a child. I don't know, but I do know that that's some wicked activity. Linda actually found this out when she had a heated argument with Helen at the Oyster House they all worked at in front of EVERYONE! How cruel can one be?

Let's switch back to her father, which was Linda's idol, and what happened to him. In the midst of growing up dysfunctional with her siblings, being an early caretaker, working as a slave, and being treated unloved, Linda was in store for something that would change her life forever. On a night least expected in Fluker, Louisiana her father was murdered by a woman right in front of her, as he was shot to death.

As if it couldn't get any worse for Linda as she laid there in her father's blood, holding him in her arms screaming to the heavens above, «Whyyyyyyy, Just WHYYYYYYY!!!» Why her father was killed is a mystery, but, I am willing to bet it had something to do with the triangle relationship affair he was in.

Linda was devastated for quite some time. As Linda became older, she and Helen had an even more painful relationship between each other following her father's death. Helen would even take Linda to the nightclubs with her as a teenager and push her towards men twice her age. I can only imagine what the rest of the siblings went through coming up as well. Helen was said to know witchcraft and practiced certain types of magic in her home.

Thinking about those birth control pills, it's not hard for me to believe she was involved in something satanic! If you would ever visit her home, you can feel a sense of «wrong spirit» in it with the black and red beads hanging through the doorways, the incense burning slowly, the dolls in each room, the dark tint and low watt lights throughout the house. Maybe, this could all be wrong but I can believe it.

As for another man being in her life, that wouldn't be the case as Helen remained a widow, living alone and, doing everything for herself. Now, as you all can see, Jasper's early life was pretty different than Linda's right? He went through some things but, he always had a loving family behind him that was taught to smile and be nice. His mother Mildred gave her last to bail him out of trouble or spoil him on many occasions.

As I write this, I feel like I'm there feeling Linda's pain growing up, but what's sad is that it didn't stop there. There will be more to come later in the story but first, let's get to the beginning of Jasper and Linda's connection. As I said before, Helen and Mildred worked together at the Oyster House and eventually, Linda and Jasper would be old enough to follow. When Jasper first laid eyes on Linda, it was one afternoon on the porch steps at Helen's house as he was walking the rock road, when he glanced at Linda in amazement and said, «You are so gorgeous, and you're going to be mine with your sexy self!»

Linda, being the person she was, just brushed that comment off and told him off quickly. Jasper was quite the comedian type, so he just laughed at her and kept walking softly saying, «I'm gonna get you woman, you watch what I tell you here.» Time passed by and the two of them started working together at the Oyster House with their parents.

So, every chance Jasper got to say some slick words to Linda, he did it persistently! It got so bad that she would throw oyster shells at him and curse him out to keep him away but, it never worked. Jasper was determined to get her. Working together caused them and their parents to become closer than just coworkers anyway so, they did end up becoming friends.

Mildred would talk to Helen regularly, sipping her Seagram's Gin, dipping snuff, as Helen smoked her cigarettes and drank her cold beers. Jasper, after some time grew tired of opening oysters, so he decided to start working at The Lallie Kemp Hospital in the kitchen. It was time for him to make money the way he wanted to but, if he needed to go back to either one in the future, he would.

Linda would stay under her mother's wing until eventually she said forget it. She found more comfort away from home in the streets. Jasper was also young and in the streets taking a little bit of his father's remedy and using it. What's amazing was that Linda ended up in a relationship with a guy named Percy while Jasper ended up with Lili Anne and a couple of other women.

At the time, Jasper was still staying with Mildred and Linda would eventually start staying with Percy. At the early stages, she felt more comfortable with him and of course, things weren't going well between her and Helen. Lili Ann moved in with Jasper for a few months under Mildred's roof and, I'm guessing Lili had problems at home as well. Mildred was a family oriented person, so opening up her home was normal.

Remember that they all had become closer than just colleagues at work. So they were all practically family; even Linda and Jasper. So, one night, Linda called Jasper and explained to him about her bad breakup with Percy; how he beat her, and how she was done with him and had nowhere to go. Jasper discussed it with Mildred who already knew about the friction between Helen and Linda, and she said, «Sure, she can come.»

Linda moves in with Mildred, Jasper, Lili Ann, and the rest of the siblings that were still staying there. Now guys understand this! Jasper has his girlfriend staying with him and his friend "Linda," that he is infatuated with! Jasper had just hit the jackpot with this one. This was on some real pimp level stuff if you ask me! As time went by, he would show Linda the kind of love her father showed her before he died. Spoiling her in ways young men at that time didn't do, and it was all so new to her.

Can you believe that Linda and Lili Ann even became friends??? They would do things together with Jasper's money, taking his car which Mildred bought him out to the clubs, and sometimes do things together. Mildred soon had to have a sit down with her son telling him, "Now, I allowed them to stay because, to me that is family but, you will not be running no hoe house in here, or you got to go son!»

To make a long story short, Linda also came to Jasper and told him he had to eventually choose between her and Lili Anne. I just knew it would get to that point though, didn't you? We all know that crazy triangle couldn't last that long and I mean guys, they were late teenagers!!! So, Jasper held on to his longtime crush Linda and told Lili Anne it was over with.

There was also some speculation about Lili and other men as well, so that made his decision much easier but, boy, Jasper was in for a treat. When he let Lili go, she was PREGNANT!!! Yes you heard me, pregnant and, she claimed to be already pregnant while she was living with him before Linda even came and she was one hundred percent sure Jasper was the father.

Linda became furious about this but, Jasper denied that the baby was his, Linda felt that the baby was made while she and Jasper were together which was so wrong in her eyes, and Lili says that she was with Jasper first so it was not wrong. Tug, Wow! It's just a big mess behind that situation with the two girls staying with you; one gets dumped finding out she's pregnant and, the other bullies her spot in Jasper's space!

A young confusing love triangle with bad results and a string of problems attached. Of course, Jasper kept messing with Lili Ann on the side of Linda along with other women but, he would always deny the allegations of him doing such. Right now, there are allegations that Jasper had a child even BEFORE Lily Anne got pregnant! Hahahaha!! AMAZING RIGHT?

Through it all, Linda would stick by Jasper's side. He was the man in her life that she had only met once before, and that was her father. You see, Jasper was a 100% man that always took care of his business. He helped Mildred pay the bills around the house (which she gave right back to him due to the trouble he was in), he spoiled Linda like she's never had, he worked all the time starting at a young age, and she was loved and protected by this young man.

You guys tell me, if she would have left him, where would she have gone? You see, this also started opening her heart to him so much that it was as if he was her father on top of being her boyfriend. That type of thinking caused her to be so crazy over him that she controlled him. Linda knew how much Jasper loved her and was crazy about her since he first laid eyes on her so, that was a wonderful advantage. She wanted him all for herself. I'm talking about the type of relationship that he can't be friends with other women, he can't be gone too long anywhere, he can't be nice as he was brought up to be, and the list goes on.

Don't get me wrong; Jasper would always be a great, funny, humorous fellow to be around but, with Linda, he couldn't be himself fully. I will get into that later on in the story because what I am telling you all connects at certain points in the story. Well, Linda and Jasper after being together in a relationship for a while, dealing with family members, and the quiet country life, they decided to move completely away to the city of New Orleans.

They wanted to try out the city life away from all the people they knew and have a fresh new start in life with just the two of them. Jasper's brother Stanford and his girlfriend Ann would also join them in New Orleans for new beginnings. Now, they learned real quickly that the city of New Orleans was no joke compared to the peaceful country. This was the party city that they fell into face first still being young with no kids (allegedly!) having a ball. They would go to the finest places all over the city, they would smoke the best weed, do heavy drugs, and Jasper would get into two times as more trouble in the streets than he did back at home.

Jasper was the hardworking smooth-talking ladies' man with that country accent different than the city talk. The police had to know his whole name in Jefferson Parish because he got in trouble a million times just for tickets alone! Mildred stayed bailing him out which caused her to become tired and move to Texas. Yes, Jasper was a woman getting trouble maker but, it never took away from his roots on what Mildred taught him.

He remained sweet, humble, and a people's person treating everyone the same. He still stuck to his roots doing a few yards for extra money and becoming a chef for a restaurant named Ground Patties. They loved him there like a piece of gold. He later learned to bartend, serve the food, and manage a team. Linda, was just as hard a worker as Jasper, working three different jobs to prove that she can be a woman and need no one else.

She was determined not to go back to the country. Her favorite job would be at the cleaners because she loved to deal with clothes. She would stand back and watch the machines in amazement because she had never seen anything like it. The customers would sometimes come in on short notice and want their attire cleaned right away after a night full of extra excitement! Linda also had two burger flipping jobs that had fluctuating schedules, so she hated those but they all paid the bills.

Speaking of bills, Linda and Jasper's first place was in the lower 9th Ward close to North Galvez Street. This was one of the toughest neighborhoods in the city, along with some of the other neighborhoods they lived in such as Fischer Projects, Algiers, Fat City, a few places across the river, and the Westbank. They moved quite a lot in the city, trying to find a place called home.

Within a short time, Jasper had seen his share of overdosed drunks bartending and, hot girls flashing their tits at him like it was Bourbon Street while Linda worked numerous hours like a slave. If she didn't work like that, she still wouldn't be comfortable because she didn't want to keep being alone at night seeing that Jasper wasn't ever there.

While Jasper was building a fan base in the nightlife working, Linda didn't have many friends and she barely talked to her family. She and her mother's relationship was still on hot coals burning slow but no matter, she loved her mama dearly, from a distance. Linda was a very secretive person which caused Jasper to be that way too. This would cause them to never have guests or visitors to their apartment!

New Orleans didn't make it any better for their trust. The crime rate was sky high, their co-workers were on drugs, they knew some people would be murdered, and some would kill like it was legal. Through it all, they never turned back to where they came from for an easier route. Some may say they were crazy for staying but, I just think with this little being said; they were two strong young people taking on life head-on with no hand outs and that's amazing.

Also, I see they didn't trust anyone, so they never invited anyone to their apartment. They should have been complimenting each other daily for making it through each storm. These two were still missing something in there life though. Still, they would check for a better environment for a real place called home to them. While they did the looking, Jasper was a wonderful caretaker of Linda but, he still couldn't leave the streets alone.

This guy was a Charlie Jackson Jr. and he had an addiction that couldn't be tamed. Linda would kick him out of the house for the hundredth time and continue to take him back. That was her daddy and soulmate guys so; it had to be tough for her.

One night stood out for Linda and Jasper out the middle of nowhere after taking a few years to do it; Jasper proposed to her in his humorous way saying, «Now woman, I want you to put this on your finger because you are mine and you ain't going nowhere damn it!» Linda looked at him full of pain in her eyes hurt from his wrongdoings and replied, «I don't want you or this damn ring so, why don't you give it to one of your floozys!»

«Honey you are the woman I want to spend the rest of my life with and, I promise you, I am done with that. I am all yours baby, now you keep that ring on your finger and give me some sugar with them lips!!» Jasper replied as he had this sneaky look on his face and no doubt any and everyone knew he loved her to death.

Linda responded as tears rolled down her face, «I love you but, you have got to get better in order for me to be here for the rest of your life.»

Of course, Jasper agreed. Linda said yes, and you won't believe where the marriage took place. In Linda's mom front yard, where only God and his angels could have arranged that. Jasper probably had to call and say a few words to Helen about what it would mean to her daughter if this could be done. So yes, their first wedding happened in Amite, Louisiana on Helen Lucky's land.

As I said, their relationship was rocky, but for this event, it could be patched up for just a second. After the wedding, the Jackson's make their way back down to the city where they would later find their apartment in Metairie, Louisiana right outside of New Orleans to claim as their place called home.

The good times would last for a short period of time as Jasper got back on a roll again in the streets. Sometimes, not coming home at all, bad association to worst friends, gambling a little, and even a lot of different types of drugs. Let's reverse back to the wedding though because I left a key part out that will make the readers scratch their heads and be amazed at how cold Jasper was.

I AM KING PART 1

We all know that receptions after weddings in the hood, can all be different where some may have a big party, some may just chat for a while, and some may just go out to the club after the wedding. Also, single women love to attend these types of events. Well guys, the Jacksons STARTED to go someplace to party on their wedding night.

The shocking part was, the Jacksons ENDED up separated at the end of the party. Brace yourselves because Jasper was the real deal with his slick ways. JASPER LEFT THE PARTY WITH TWO WOMEN GUYS!! Yes, you heard me. He left with two women on his arm that night and god knows what happened. But in today's society, he'd probably end up missing for good!!!

Who in their right mind can do something like that right after their wedding? Jasper is the only answer I can give you. I do not know what the excuse was for getting back in with Linda, but once again he had his way. The smooth-talking daddy Mack got back into the ball game to win her heart but, I will never know how. Let's just blame it on drugs and being very young I would say.

With all that being said, the Jackson's were trying once again for a while now and were ready for the next biggest step in their lives, a child. Well, at least Jasper was very eager to have a son to teach the same things he was taught and to become better than he was. On the other hand, Linda deep down inside, wanted a family but was scared of Jasper's wrongdoings, of her problems, and how strict she knew she would be because of the way she was raised.

Linda shut Jasper down every time he would ask, but she loved that man, so they tried numerous times. He was still a man in the streets and she was still a working woman dealing with Jasper on one side and her family issues as well. Jasper's side of the family, on the other hand, was always supportive of him and they were still close. Mildred would stay on Jasper about being a better man to be able to raise a son and to not follow in Charlie's footsteps but to always love him no matter what.

The Jacksons stayed in a hood but the better part of the city now. They were married in God's eyes, and they had both become eager to have a child, girl or boy. Well finally, all of that trying worked for the Jacksons. A few months later, a little baby was born in Jefferson Parish on an early August morning. As she smiled nervously, Linda laid there holding their baby in her arms as Jasper stood over the both of them and said, «I got my baby boy. Thank you so much God!»

Linda looks up at Jasper slowly, rolling her eyes and smiling at the same time as she replied gently glancing back at her son saying, «Yea, maybe now your daddy will act right. You, on the other hand, are my big ole boy and we will give you a name from the Bible because you are a special child.

Someone that will grow to lead people of all kinds and create a better life than I had, just like the good book says!» Linda and Jasper glanced at each other slowly and, as they both looked back at their newly born son, Jasper gave him a powerful name. As the baby opened his eyes, Jasper proudly said, «Hey there my son, your name will be... JOSHUA!"

CHAPTER 2

BABY JOSHUA

"Birth is a heaven-given right for every baby."
– Toba Beta

On August 23, 1986, at approximately 4:30 am in the Jefferson Parish of New Orleans, Joshua Demetrius Jackson took his first breath! Linda and Jasper had finally got what they've wished for. Jasper could not take the smile off of his face, as Joshua laid there trying to get a feel for the world he just became a part of. As a few days passed, they were able to take baby Joshua to their apartment home in Metairie, La.

With time, Linda and Jasper started to understand that raising a child and parenting can be a very tough ball lifestyle change. Learning how to feed Joshua, change his diaper, bath him, protect him, and how to have patience. You have to remember that these two were in the city all on their own, they worked like crazy, and they were still young adults.

Now, what's crazy about this is that Jasper was out still doing his dirt in the streets having no limits but, he loved his son Joshua. Any and everywhere Jasper went, he would take Joshua along with him. Now in this chapter, I will be going forward in time a bit so stay with me. Now, when I say Jasper took Joshua everywhere, I really meant EVERYWHERE. Jasper at the time was heavy into drugs so, he would go a few places to use or to buy the product whether it be weed, crack cocaine, pills or anything to get a quick high.

While doing so, Jasper would take Joshua with him on his dirty runs! If the child protective services would have found out about the wrongdoings of Jasper, exposing his son to that type of environment, only God knows the consequences. I wouldn't dare say that Jasper did anything to hurt Joshua or endanger him on purpose, but it sure does seem that way when you read this. Understand guys that Joshua was a little older at the time this is taking place.

He was about three to four years old now and very intelligent at that age. These drug houses are nowadays referred to as "Trap Houses" or "Bandos" in the lower class areas of the city. Well, as a growing baby, Joshua would start to experience the life of the hood. Can you close your eyes and picture being a young baby boy, sitting on the hood of a car outside a trap house for hours, crackheads walking around like zombies and your father inside not even understanding the seriousness of his son being outside alone at that time? Can You?

Kidnap, rape, child protective services, killed, or anything that comes to one's mind about what could have happened to Joshua! This was one of the worst cities in the U.S. when it comes to murder rate and crime at the time!! Linda, on the other hand, is either at home, at one of her jobs, or a slot machine with a cigarette in her mouth trying to win big. I would imagine as a mother she'd probably have a heart attack if she had known any of this went on, numerous times.

That would be tough for Linda to find any of it out seeing that Jasper was a smooth person and she also had no thought in her mind that Jasper would do anything like this around their child you know. So that alone helped Jasper on all the getaway activities he may have, by using his son. Crack rock would be running through his father's veins, stoned out his mind while being driven around the city of New Orleans on his way to a side chick's house to lay up!

Now maybe Jasper's actions did seem messed up but he meant no harm. In fact, Joshua actually spent more time under Jasper than his mother. As a baby boy, whether he was smart or not, Joshua had no clue with what was going on around him. In his eyes, all he saw was his father being not just a dad but his friend. Jasper would sit him down at the end of his bed personally on a weekly basis and say, "Son, you are the greatest thing that has ever happened to me besides your mother. Now, of course, I do some things that you don't quite understand just yet but, I just want you to know that I will never do anything to hurt you."

"I do some very bad things, and I stay gone for long periods of time but, I want you to know that we are all we have. You are a very intelligent son, and even at your age, I can tell that one day you will be 'king of the jungle' doing things you can't even imagine yet! I love you my son."

When Joshua hears things like this from his father as a child, although he was young, you better believe it would stick to him like glue. In Joshua's eyes, Dad could do no wrong because the little things that were shared with him drew his heart closer to his Dad. Linda, on the other hand, never said I love you, never had a sit-down talk, and was always mad at something. So, when little Joshua would be in the projects seeing things he shouldn't, maybe looking out the window waiting for Dad to pull up, or just believing Dad when he would promise him something that never happened, he would always have this special love for Jasper no matter what.

Now, parenting for Linda wasn't a cup of hot tea either. You all read a glimpse of her history with her parents which was terrifying. Joshua was pretty much in the hands of two young people that loved him true enough but had a puzzling way of showing it. When he had his times with his mother, it wouldn't be a perfect connection at all. It would be mostly yelling, slaps in the face, and if Josh cried about anything, he would get put in a dark room with the door shut, to cry himself to sleep!

The slaps to the face would be Linda's signature move towards her son. Anyways, since they couldn't always afford daycare, Joshua had to go with Linda to her jobs and sit in the back until she finished her shifts overnight. His dad, would either be at work or not heard from for a while so, Linda had to do what was best in her eyes. Sometimes, it would get so bad that Josh would have to sit with Linda like a grown up, watching her play slots for money from evening until morning!!! Guys this is a heck of a life for a toddler!

As you read, you can reflect and understand that this was all a part of a generational curse. Jasper's father ran the streets and so did he. His uncles did drugs, so he endeavored in the same, if not harder drugs. He drank Seagram's Gin like his mother Mill, He worked as a slave never being lazy, and he still was passionate, and loving like his grandfather.

He had his flaws but, he had love in his heart, and that's what set him apart from Linda as far as the generational curse. In God's name, Linda was mad 90 percent of the time like her mother's identical twin. She was emotional 5 percent of the time and, the other 5 percent left, she tried her hardest to smile and be different from her mother. That was her toughest break though, but the positive about her was that she was a workaholic, she took care of her husband, and she wanted to change.

She had very tough skin and had been through too much too early to break the curses. Poor baby Joshua would suffer for all that she had been and was going through. When his parents were in good terms and not arguing, they would go out, take trips, and do things recreational without Josh. He was told that they didn't need kids around them when they are trying to have fun. He was a child that didn't go anywhere unless it was the local park on a few occasions, the slot machines with his mother, or not so good places with his dad.

He did go to some different daycares day and night though. That was when he got to experience being around other people for the first time. As he got older; around four years of age, he started going through a lot at home but he was getting smarter as well. One of the things we will get into details later is that Joshua didn't eat much at home and he was only allowed to eat certain foods due to his mother's demons.

So, he would take full advantage at the daycares getting fed extra food either by the sitters or the other kids there. No one ever knew what he was going through because he was taught always to be quiet, have no friends, and never trust anyone. Crazy life for a growing boy in the city of New Orleans I tell you!

Although some summers, he was allowed to visit his grandmother Helen in the country, it still would be weird because his mother and Helen were still at odds. This would be the 5 percent of good in Linda's heart to let him go! The most monumental moments in Joshua's life were the times away from his parents. A break well needed at such a young age woooo!!

Summers in the country were some of the best times of Joshua's life. Being able to experience the freedom to play out in the sun with no worries of anything bad happening. Back at home, due to the level of crime, it would be tough for Josh to play outside or have friends while listening to Linda yap about everything. Life in the country with grandma was a different life though. Josh would be able to sleep longer, eat whatever he wanted, and play as long as he wanted to!

He witnessed real life of a child growing up at that age in a normal state. He would also be accompanied by his little cousin Anastasia Jackson better known as Stacy. Now on a quick note, he actually had more cousins that would hang around a little, like Ellis and Eric Taylor, Michael and Evette Wilson, Pudden, Walter Mason, and a few more from Bennet Road, but he and Stacy would be the main duo.

Besides Stacy, Michael would also be a big addition in Joshua's life at the time, but the others were so spoiled it was hard for a boy like Josh to relate so they didn't hang much. So anyways, Helen would sit back, drink her cold beers, and smoke her cigarettes calling them her grandbabies. Josh and Stacy, were really tight like a sister and a brother doing everything together. Every single day you could smell the aroma of sausage, eggs, bacon, pancakes, and grits with butter early in the morning which was Joshua's favorite.

Then, at nightfall, something different would be cooked up for dinner that smelled just as good as the morning! He didn't know what dinner was where he was from. He barely even ate at home. Stacy would always get in trouble by Helen because she never ate all of her food. She was into snacks; she was spoiled and, the only child at the time, so regular food wasn't her thing. Joshua, on the other hand loved anything you put in front of him except vegetables, candy, and sweets. Linda didn't allow him to eat any sweets like the rest of the kids.

Also, he was trained to eat all of his food on his plate and if there's any leftover on the stove to eat that also. His Granny would look in amazement loudly saying, "Boy you got a damn tapeworm don't you? They must not have been feeding my big boy down there?" Even at that age, Joshua wasn't dumb enough to answer that honestly, so he just dropped his head and kept eating.

"Yea, I know that daughter of mine ain't doing you right down there, you don't have to say anything but God don't like ugly!" Helen said as she shook her head and puffed her cigarette. Joshua was smart enough to understand who showed more love towards him. But what he couldn't understand is why both didn't treat him the same along with other questions his small brain held. Nonetheless, Josh and his only friend/cousin would go tear up some stuff some more and have a great time.

Now, these two children were very smart to be four and five years of age, and Helen treated them that way. The reason why I said this though is because besides the fun, the great food, and the different life for Joshua, he learned so much from his grandmother Helen as she talked to them like young adults. Helen had a thing about talking to her grandchildren about her own children weirdly and negatively.

When you are a toddler, you soak things in like a sponge, especially if it's your mom's mother. In the next chapter of this book, you'll find out that Joshua was a child that did not grow to have birthdays, Christmas, candy, friends, recreation, and the list goes on. I said that to give your mind an image of your grandmother telling you these things at that age and blaming it all on your mother, which is her daughter.

This is what Joshua would hear at the time but mind you, he is only a toddler and he has no idea of the relationship differences between his mother and Helen. All he sees is that mother treats him terrible at home along with a good/dangerous father that promises to take him one place but wounds up somewhere else every time. On the other hand, he sees grandmother Helen in a totally different perspective because she provides everything he was missing at home.

So basically, if she talks negatively to Joshua about his mother, well hey, so be it because he was having more fun in the country anyhow. In the midst of doing that, statements would be made in a positive way about Stacy's mother that was kind of confusing to Joshua for a split second because Stacy's mother was the baby to Helen so, she could never do any wrong for some reason. She would always speak highly of her and really low about Linda as if she hated her. So yes, little Joshua had an idea of it, heard a lot at that age, but couldn't quite put it all together at the time.

Meanwhile, he was living his life and he felt like what Helen was saying was true, so he had no intentions of going back home. Joshua had finally had a friend to play with in cousin Stacy, acres of land to be a kid on, and a grandmother that served great food helping him gain tons of weight, this was the life! You would think when you hear the word summer, that it was a long two to three months but, Joshua would only have the luxury of staying two weeks at a time.

Two weeks would be the longest country getaways to him and he would enjoy every minute. The tension between mother and daughter shortened his time away from home. Linda would always call with an aggravated tone, "You ready to come home yet boy?" Joshua would reply as a tear slowly dropped down his cheek, "No mama can I stay a little longer?" Helen and Stacy would sit back and listen to Linda's loud voice through the phone telling him, "No the hell you cannot and don't you ask me no damn more, you've been gone long enough!"

Joshua would leave into the other room, crawl into the bed, and lay there squeezing the pillow crying softly until his mother showed up. After about two hours, Linda showed up and talked to her mother as if there were no tension between the two of them. Then snatches Joshua out of the room. As they put their seatbelts on in the car, she turns around and tells him, "You better stop playing with me before I slap you in your face, you know you're not staying over there long! She probably talked about me the whole time and I'm her damn daughter!

You going to get home, do some cleaning, and go to that back room, you've had enough fun!"

You would think Joshua was on punishment the way he was treated – in the middle of a daughter/mother crossfire, which each of them seemed to go to him with the problems instead of addressing each other. This was a young boy suffering the consequences of others' actions! Well, it was back on the Causeway Bridge towards home – sweet hell again! While on the bridge, Joshua would stare nonstop at the water and blue skies thinking of all sorts of things the normal kids don't think about.

The little houses on the water, the birds flying high above, the thought of what was living in the water, and numerous visions controlling his mind. Finally, making it back to New Orleans, Joshua would go into the back room with his Ninja Turtle toy box, box-shaped T.V. with aluminum foil on the antenna that didn't work, his books including the Bible, the rats in the walls, the flying roaches, and his hard bunk bed mattress to lay and think like that of Albert Einstein.

At such a young age, he would lay there and have a mind full of thoughts majority of older people may think of! Joshua would read scriptures out of the Bible he got from his grandmother, all by himself, over and over again. He would also slowly start putting things together in his own way with his Father ways of loving him, the things that were said about his Mother from his Grandmother, the different lives his country cousins had, the puzzled way he was treated, the fun he had with Stacy, the smell from the breakfast his grandma cooked, and the list goes on.

He would lay there listening to the other children play outside, the basic TV. playing in the other room that he wasn't allowed to watch, and the food that was cooking from his mother knowing that he wouldn't be fed any of it. His mind had started to develop quicker than the average child because he didn't do what the other kids did. His life and thought process was different from everything around him.

For instance, consider someone blind. It is said that a blind person cannot see, but their other senses such as touch and hearing are so much better than everyone else; since their vision is absent, those other senses become stronger. Well, take this illustration and compare it to Joshua. It was like being blind to what regular children did around him, so that caused other abilities in him to become stronger just as a blind person.

It cost him a life without a childhood though, which also played a big part in Joshua feeling so alone. He was the only baby boy in the house growing quicker than ever. At this point, he could comprehend almost anything that was put in front of him. Meanwhile, it's time for another birthday for Joshua without any type of party to celebrate it. Joshua was poor living in a lower class area so, even if his mom was touched by God to be nice, he still couldn't receive anything because of their money situations.

This particular birthday was different though guys. As Joshua sat in a small corner in the back room, he heard a knock at the door as the television in the living room was muted. His mother got up mumbling, "Who in the hell is this white lady?" Although it was a few days before "Happy Birthday" to Joshua! As his mother opened the door, he peeked through a crack in the room quietly listening.

The lady gently smiled and said, "Hello!! My name is Mrs. Kilcrease, and I teach pre-k students in school. Here is all the info you need to put your son into school early at his age. Thank you for your time Mrs. Jackson and I'll see you soon!" His life was changing with age and headed towards education. It was now time to move on to a new chapter in his life from a baby, into a young boy… GOING TO SCHOOL!

CHAPTER 3

THE DEVELOPING OF A GROWING BOY

"If the boy feels safe, he can take risks, ask questions, make mistakes, learn to trust, share his feelings, and grow
- Alfie Kohn

(STORY WILL NOW BE TOLD IN THE FIRST PERSON)

As my alarm clock rang constantly, I jumped quickly down my bunk bed to turn off the aggravating noise. It was November in Kenner, Louisiana on Huntsville Street, cool and foggy outside, quiet in my room, and cold on my feet as I stood there trying to wake up. We had moved from Metairie, La due to money issues. I was five years old at the time and I was already waking myself up for school. That's right; I was in school all grown up now!

I had been attending West Gate Maggiore for a couple of months now in Mrs. Kilcrease's class. For the most part, I would wake myself up for school because my parents believed it was my responsibility. Now, of course, the first day of school, my mother walked me to the bus stop and took a picture, but the rest was history. Linda would never come to the bus stop, a school event, or just to see how I was doing in school ever again.

Weird, but I guess life goes on right. So, as I got dressed every morning at the same time, I could hear our next door neighbors rapping, smoking weed, or passing around a bottle of Old English 800. My slide window in the back room was located right next to where they would hang out, and I would always peak my head out to listen to them.

As I did so, they would always say the same thing, "Hey lil JJ WASSSAMMM WITH YOU WODIE! Take a shot of this OE before you go to school ya heard me!" I would look at them, wave, and smile as I closed my window to start getting dressed. I was shy, so I never talked much at all or showed much emotion. I wasn't the average five year old seeing that I would actually dress myself; tying my shoes, buttoning my shirt, and putting on my pants.

I didn't have many clothes to choose from and only one pair of shoes, so that made it much easier to do it all myself. As I brushed my teeth, I gazed at the mirror thinking, thinking, and thinking even more – thoughts I seemed to have no control over — confusing pictures in my mind, situations that have happened, and thoughts of what is to come.

Sometimes, I would have to snap myself out of those thoughts! As I finished up, I grabbed my backpack slowly coming out of my room looking around, staring at my mom and dad's room because, I wasn't allowed to go into it, due to privacy reasons wondering if one of them was home, and finally, I just took off out the door. Not your typical 5-year-old getting ready for school story right!!!

Well the one vehicle we did have was gone from its parking spot so; I had no idea who was home and who was gone. At the time, my parents worked a lot, whether it was night shifts, doubles, or mornings when I had to go to school. This situation was so illegal, but being home alone didn't bother me. Anyways, as I walk out the door, I got persuaded easily by my neighbors to come over and take a sip of their OE. They claimed it took the worms out of my stomach hahaha!!!

Then, I went to the bus stop right up the street at the stop sign. By the time I made it to the bus stop with the rest of the kids on the block, I was already woozy from that drink. I would always see my mother and father drink it, so I didn't see anything harmful about it. When the bus came, I went straight to the back, never talked to anyone, and fell asleep. Believe it or not guys, this was my school wake up routine for quite some time.

As we pull up to the school, I was the last to get off the bus. I would sometimes look at the mothers that dropped their children off, kiss them, fix their clothes or tell them I love you. This was a hood school but affection was still shown so, at the time, I was puzzled because I didn't get that at home. I felt distant and different from a lot of the kids in my school. They wore their nice shoes with matching clothes and walked into the school with friends as I walked alone.

But I tell you one thing; I love breakfast and lunch at school because I stayed hungry, eating it all while sitting alone at the end of the table. Being only five years old, it didn't all click too well to me yet. Perfect example, as I went through my day in school, for one hour out of each day, I had a mysterious second teacher. I was the only student that was assigned to her. It would be more like a questionnaire with her than a class.

What I mean is, she would ask me tons of questions as I colored and read books. "How are you feeling today Joshua? Are you happy? How is your life at home? What would you like to be when you grow up?" The list goes on and on with numerous questions she would ask. These were called our sessions with my counselor. As she directs me back to my classroom, she would always stop me in the hallway, squat down and tell me, "If you need anything or if you ever want to talk, I'm here Joshua!"

I got into my class and took a seat. About thirty minutes into class, though it would be Mat (sleep) time where all of us would have to go to sleep on our mats. As the lights dimmed and everyone slept, I would lie there with my eyes open thinking as always. What was Mrs. Lady talking about, seeing that I never remembered her name? I couldn't go home and ask my parents because I was trained not to ask them questions on certain things, but what's funny is, they raised me to come to them about any and everything I knew.

Just really weird and confusing if you ask me. Well, it was time for us to get up from the mats and load up the school buses as we were escorted by our teachers to get on. On the way home, I would always look out the window as we rolled down Veterans Memorial through traffic just looking at the world in my view. People honking their horns, the police pulling someone over, the ambulance zooming by or the different places and stores I've never been able to visit yet.

As we pull up at the cross street of Huntsville, I got off the bus and slowly walked home paying attention to everything in my view. One neighbor would always be cooking something on his barbecue grill listening to blues. The next neighbors were a bunch of hard heads fighting their pit bulls while smoking weed, and of course, right next to my house the Old English sipping guys were still at it playing dominoes now. "You back huh JJ? Did you learn anything, I hope so, because these streets ain't nothing nice little one," they replied. As I walked into the house, I nodded at them and closed the door behind me. My mother had curtains over the blinds, so it'll be pretty dark as I walked in. I know for a fact that my mother would be sleeping because she came back home this morning and she would have to go back again tonight. I usually go with her to work because my father worked nights as well or sometimes doesn't come home for a couple of days, which was a normal routine.

Well, as I moved to switch the lights on, roaches scattered everywhere and at the same time, a huge rat ran across my foot! My God, I've lost count on how many times that has happened and I still get the chills thinking about it! As the rat ran across my foot, I screamed at the top of my lungs and this woke up the beast, my mother, Hahahahaha.

"Boy, what in the hell you screaming like that for? You should be used to the damn things by now," she replied as she ran out of her room in shock.

"Now sit down at the damn table and get your homework out, and you ain't give that teacher no hard time today, did you?" She asked aggressively. "No ma'am, I was good," I replied as I still looked around for the critters! The roaches and rats were bad business in our house! They even came to school with me coming all out of my clothes or my backpack. No matter what hood we lived in or where we would move to, they would follow.

For now though, they were gone, so my mother and I could do my homework. If there's anything great I could say about my mother, she sure knew how to teach me reading, speech, English, and spelling. It's because of her I could read any book at that age, spell any word; although I was shy, I could stand in front of people and talk with ease. I took numerous beatings with plug-in cords and switches until I bled with swollen wounds but that was the only way she knew how to teach me.

I would stand on my feet for hours practicing different hand gestures as she beat my hands if I got lazy or tired! I wouldn't wish that on any child but the brutal teaching would later on help me in life I guess. Once we get done with my homework, we had to leave and go to Dunkin Donuts since I woke her up too early. We sure weren't going there to eat though; I can tell you that. My mom hated her night job, which was McDonalds. So anything she could do to get away from there, she would try. Dunkin Donuts wasn't too far from her job, so she would always stop there because back in the day, they had money slot machines.

Now, I could be wrong on the name Dunkin Donuts, but I promise you, there was a big-time donut shop with slot machines closed off by black pull back curtains. The workers knew me and my mother by name – we came so much! I remember begging my mother for quarters to play the arcade machines as she played on the slots. I only got to play a few times seeing that every quarter counts for her and her slot chances. As I would sit there waiting for her, the smell of fresh donuts would go all the way down to my tummy while I could hear her cursing the machines out for no reason, not caring for once about a donut.

I was hungry, bored, and very uncomfortable in there, but it had begun to be a part of our life and routine. My mother would sometimes walk out from behind the curtains and I would jump up only to see her go to the counter to turn in a ticket that allows her to play some more! Sometimes, we would even be late for her job because she believed she would someday hit big in there I guess.

So finally, we headed to her job after she had lost a good bit of money. As she looks at me still pissed she said, "Now when we get in here, I'm going to sit you in the back of my office so don't you make one sound you hear me!" I always nodded my head and just replied a soft ok. I remained seated in that back room for hours! It felt like child imprisonment with a very small television that barely had a connection with little black and white beads running through it like the one I had in the backroom!

Somehow, I made it through this situation many times. I've heard and seen the most amazing things a child should not witness at all. I guess that's why at such a young age, I was very much advanced in my mind. But to many, it probably didn't seem that way due to my shy actions. I always paid close attention to everything that would go on, no matter how small or big it was. My mother had to be a manager of some type because she ran that place and everyone in it.

The drive through would move constantly, the grill would move quickly, and the front counter was like clockwork with my mother pushing everyone. I remember vividly one night I was asleep in the back and all of a sudden, I was awoken by shouts of fire in the McDonalds parking lot! Everyone dropped to the floor as well as my mother! I was stuck in the back as my mother screamed to me, "Get down Joshua!"

I did the opposite as I slowly peeped out the window right next to the office. I look to see one vehicle flying out of the parking lot, one guy lying on the ground as blood flowed everywhere, and a lady on her knees holding the man crying. Although I was confused, I noticed the guy wasn't moving at all. "Didn't I tell you to get your ass down damn it," my mother shouted as she snatched me and threw me into the office and locked the door.

From that point on, I heard a lot of mumbling, sirens, and loud talking but I was pretty much out of the situation. I had never seen anything like it and it would just add to the many questions I had going on in my mind already. Finally, when everything was over, we would head home. My mother was quite the whole time smoking cigarettes back to back with tears running down her eyes. You remember earlier in the story about what happened to her father right?

I imagine this incident made her reflect on him or even being worried about my father being in the streets like he was. So, as we were almost home, I looked at my mother and asked her something that shocked her, "Mama was that Cain and Abel's descendants? In the Bible, it reads that one brother killed the other brother and that the living brother later has family descendants." As my mother listened, she was amazed by my intelligence and replied softly, "No Joshua, it was nothing serious tonight, so just focus on your reading more."

As I looked out the window, I knew my mother was lying to me. It didn't take a rocket scientist to know that he was dead! The rest of the night, even when we made it home, she was silent and went straight to her room closing the door behind her. I had never seen my mother have emotions before besides going crazy over my father. Well, as days, weeks, and months went by, that routine was frequent and even stayed with her at the workplace. On her off days, she would be waiting for me to get out of school so we can hit that donut shop wide open and I hated it hahaha!!

The weekends were different though because I got to hang out with my father more – being in those sinful places with him. Often, we would go under the bridge in New Orleans to the park and when I tell you everybody from every hood was out there like a celebration. Second lines would be formed where people would dance and sing. Barbecuing would be done along with a few disagreements, fights, and shooting once again.

For the most part, it was something to experience. Also, Mardi Gras was me and my father's second home even as I grew up. We would wake up early in the morning to catch everything so we wouldn't miss any of the festivities. "Throw me something Mister!" I would yell at the top of my lungs as my father held me on his shoulders. My mother barely came with us to Fat Tuesday and Mardi Gras but my father and I had a blast every year!

Life was truly an experience for me, tough at times, and a bit puzzling, but will only get a bit more interesting and tough for me as I get older. There was a new chapter in my life that was forming into some painful challenges that the majority of children wouldn't be able to endure. As I write, I noticed that my story was becoming better but harder to go back and revisit. Let's go a little deeper in the next chapter shall we...

CHAPTER 4

THE PAINFUL CHALLENGES

"Someday everything will make perfect sense. So for now, laugh at the confusion, smile through the tears, and keep reminding yourself that everything happens for a reason!"
- John Mayer

On Christmas Eve, as I stood there looking at the tree full of lights, I noticed there were two or three presents under the tree. In full amazement, I saw my name on one of the wrappers and I immediately opened it! Now, I was smart, so I knew I would receive consequences for this, but I didn't care! As I tore the wrapping paper, I pulled out a huge redshirt twice my size, and I put it on. We all know that was not a typical childhood present but I never got anything before so to me, it was like candy to a baby.

I wore it all around the house that day, seeing that I was there all alone because my mother was at work and my father was working as well, I think. Although I was told never to open the door, I did anyway just to be nosey on the day before Christmas. As I stood there on the balcony stairs of the apartments, I can see the families all getting ready for Christmas, the children playing in the yard, decorations on the run down hood houses, and the list goes on.

I would sit there for quite some time, asking myself; why wouldn't all my family members come together like that? I was so confused about what was taking place in my life at the time and things weren't getting any better either.

Well, as I was sitting there being nosey, my mother pulled up having gotten off early from work saying, "Boy what the hell did I tell you about coming outside when we're not home? You're trying to get us in trouble damn it! I know good and damn well you took that present and opened it! How the hell you know that was for you, it coulda been for another Joshua we know! Take your tail in that room right now because it ain't your room; you're just living here, and take off all them clothes stupid ass!"

As I go to my room crying heavily at the crucial words that came out her mouth, I would sit there in a confusing manner puzzled as hell. Even though I knew I had consequences, what did I do so wrong to her were my thoughts. Why can't I call this my room, why am I stupid, and why does she keep slapping me in my face with her bare hand making me feel pain?

As I sat down naked, waiting, she came into the room with a black cord! When she was done beating and slandering me with words, I would have to go to bed once again, hungry. I was just a kid going through the most. I had been whipped like an African slave, but the confusing words hurt me the most. It should have been like second nature to me now because I heard it from her mouth so much.

The amazing part about events like this is that my father was barely home to witness it and if he was home, he wouldn't do anything but let it happen to me or join in on whipping me, while he was stoned out of his mind. He had so much going on that he didn't notice my pain at all, or at least at the time I didn't think he did. He would sometimes come in early in the morning and slip me some food that he had left over from his job.

I guess that's probably why I used to stay up waiting on him constantly starving and sometimes he wouldn't show. I learned to realize that all the frustration from my mom's mother, her jobs, and my father's wrongdoings, would all be taken out on me! Not a fair life at all for any child. Well, on Christmas Day, I wasn't too fond of it, seeing that every one of them were just not right for me at all.

Now, the good thing is we did go to the country to see my grandmother every year and eat up everything, but they still had drama between each other as well. I remember my next Christmas, I received a Sega Genesis and at the time that game console was very popular. It even came with the Sonic the Hedgehog game already, and boy was I excited! I told my mother that I loved her to death that day, and she looked at me while grinning but she didn't tell me back.

It didn't matter to me though because I thought I was on top of the world once in my little life at the time! Sad to say that the following day after Christmas, my mother took the game console back to the store because we needed the money I guess. I never even hooked the game up, much less play it! "Here we go again," I thought as I was heartbroken and lost in my mind! My grandmother talked bad about her again; they got into their usual spat, and back on our way we were presentless.

Such a crushing point in my life started to develop into a trend. Similar to birthdays, I only received one party around the age of three, surrounded by Bennett Rd cousins and family I barely ever hung around! It was official in my mind that Santa didn't think I was nice, and my growing of age did not mean much for a birthday. Now, not only did these type of days affect my life at home, but it was punishing me at school as well.

I was the butt joke at school; so bad to the point that I hated going! Children would come to school loaded with presents, projects, goodies, etc. all geared towards holiday events. Getting a hug or love from their parents or even if it was just walking in with their family members to school, I was the total opposite. I had nothing to show for and the kids would use me as a comedy show, to laugh all day long.

Although it was going on for a long time now, it still never got old and I could never get used to the painful words. Even when it wasn't holidays, on a regular day, I'll get pushed around and picked on – for my dirty shoes, smelly cigarette clothing, crooked teeth, and rat holes in my clothes, or even for not having friends. Don't let me get the baby from the king cake around February seeing that New Orleans tradition was whomever grabbed the baby out, has to bring the next cake to school.

The cake from me would never be seen because we had no money at home and if we did, my mother and father had habits that affected my childhood tremendously. At some point in my childhood life, I became a different person full of confusion. I started to look for bad things to happen to me. I started to feel that what other students and my mother would slander me with, were true. My most comfortable place had become my room with my ninja turtle toy box full of pencils, paper, books and little toys my grandmother sent me earlier in my life.

This would become my safe haven. I became immune to my mother's frustration, although it still all hurt, I could handle it better now that I'm around eight or nine years of age. As I sat on the floor of my room writing, I could see the shadow of mother's feet slowly walking past the door, like I was in some horror movie. I would shiver when I felt she was coming into my room or when she called my name aggressively to come do my chores.

I felt like Cinderella always cleaning up except, I was all alone. I had become a different child at school being used to not having anything or picked on daily. It had become life to me. One time I remember like yesterday, I was sitting in the classroom. As I put my backpack down on the side of my desk and opened it just slightly with the zipper, a baby rat came out and it freaked out the entire classroom! My day couldn't have gotten any worse because the whole school knew by the end of the day and even the teachers looked at me outrageously knowing they had rats at their homes as well probably!

At least I hoped they did! Not to mention, the same thing happened to me with a roach, but I was able to catch that one with my foot before it shocked the classroom. In the back room, I would feel so alone that I would talk to myself as I write words down on paper while sitting on the floor. I would write down all that's happening in my little life at the time.

The words my mother would tell me, the things she would do to me due to her anger, and the school life that I hated to go back to. I asked myself questions; was my life going to be trapped in a room, why don't I see my father much, and why he feeds me while my mother barely does, he shows me love and comes to my school but she never does any of that. At this point, I don't like where my life is at as a kid and I'm too young to understand if I deserve it or not.

Childhood wasn't a part of my life much then. When I got home from school, I would have those Cinderella chores from my mother, but if my father was around, I'd wound up having blisters in my little hands from the yard work we did. Anything from raking, mowing, cutting trees, pulling grass from flower beds, or hauling dirt! He would put the lawn mower in the back of his trunk and the other equipment in the back seat because he didn't have a truck yet. We worked some nights if he came home and most weekends. As time went by, I realized yard work was my father's passion and even though it hurt my childhood, I learned a lot from him.

I learned how to work nonstop, take pain, the power of self-employment, being my own boss and the ladies reaction to it all. "Now son, I have to make a stop over here in the 17th Ward but you can come in with me ok," my father said as I look at him smiling lightly. You see, I've already been through this with him since the beginning like I told you. He was dating a side chick in the lower 17th Ward and he forced me in the middle of it! It was a very small run down home that looked similar to the trap houses I would be at with him.

As I sat on the couch, my father went into the other room covered by a thin sheet, without a door. You could hear him talking to someone and suddenly a lady came from behind the curtain and said, "Hey there Joshua! I've heard a lot about you because your father brags about you all the time. I would love to get you a Gameboy for your birthday if you would let me, so just think about it ok?" I looked up at her with a smile and nodded my head as my response.

She also told me that she and my father were just friends and I shouldn't be nervous at all, as she walked back behind the sheet over the doorway. I laid there on the couch for about an hour and a half. My father peeked his head from behind the curtain and said, "We gonna roll to Kenner to Check IN/Check Out for a big po-boy before they close ok son!" I would just look at him and nod my head.

Just as I had thought he was going to do, he lied and we went home after he was done. As we pull up in the driveway, he looked at me with a 'high as a kite grin' on his face, and said to me, "Son you won't ever tell on your daddy would you? I love your mama to death, so when we go inside, I just want you to tell her we stopped together at the park to spend some time ok."

As we walk into the house, I slowly walked to the bathroom to take a bath because I felt like an old man very sore and tired from all the work we had done earlier that day. As I finished, sure enough, as soon as I walked into my 'jail cell' of a room, there goes mother dearest asking questions about my father. Lucky for him, he was already gone either for an overnight job, or God knows where. Well, when about 5 minutes had passed, all you could hear would be another beating. Guys this life was a monthly routine for me added to any other. I had never snitched on my father and his wrongdoings. In return, I was beaten to a pulp, while I had my problems at home that he didn't have a clue about! I know it's weird, but I started to get used to going with him though and actually a relief away from my mother despite the consequences.

As long as my father kept sober while working, he was all about that million dollar smile and enthusiasm! I could never stay mad at him long at all. I learned that he had a gift about him that my mother couldn't get away from either. I remember hearing it out her mouth saying, "God, why can't I just get rid of this man because I'm so sick and tired of his shit!" I was soft for my father, but as I write this book, I am understanding that although I was terrified of my mother, she had her reasons for doing some terrible things to me due to her frustration.

I still feel that there will never be a good enough excuse for the way she treated me but she was dogged out by the people she loved the most as well. I can say for rainy days alone; she would pull out that bottle of Old English malt liquor and pour me a small cup of it and say, "Sit at this table and drink with me!" I would do exactly as she said with the quickness too. "Damn boy, you sho is running to this drink pretty fast! Don't let me catch you taking no sips out of this bottle hea, and you don't belong in that refrigerator Nooo!"

I would just nod my head, as I sipped my drink, thinking about how much of a veteran I was at this point due to my neighbors letting me sip every morning. Meanwhile, every time she made it to her tipsy stage, she would make us root beer floats with lays potato chips. I would think to myself that it's times like this, that I know somewhere deep in her, she had a heart or it was just the drink and weed working in her brain.

Laying in the back room now, I look up at the ceiling as it was pitch dark. Speaking of the dark, I wasn't accustomed to light in my room because my mother told people that as a baby when I cried and didn't stop, she would put me in a pitch dark room to show me a lesson about crying. That's why light has never been a priority to me. I never watched television growing up either because their room had the working TV. and mine had a small box television with aluminum foil on the antenna, with roaches crawling out the back of it. At this point, it was regular life to me and I felt like just what I was, another boy in the hood getting by, but not the average.

The only difference was, I became totally different from other kids. Their troubles weren't like mine, their parents were way different, and they had a childhood. Even if they just had a mother and their fathers were absent in their lives, I felt that they still had life ten times better than mine! I started to bottle all these things in that I was going through, emotions I was feeling, the uncalled for beatings, the other kids' life vs mine, my school troubles, my restrictions in the house barely even getting to use the bathroom down to not being able to call a room that I slept in mine, my father never being here for me unless it's to take me on a crack or hoe run, or work me like a Hebrew in the heat, and the list kept piling up!

I AM KING PART 1

Now at this point in my life, I pretty much got to the basics of what I went through personally, but there were still some questionable things that were just out of my control. The first thing is the damn counselor lady who was still around and I'm like nine years old at this point. Secondly, I have another person counselor/doctor after school that they take me to that checks my body out and questions me at least once a week. When I say, for this certain doctor, my mother acted like Jesus was right in front of her. She would lie to the people and smile from ear to ear but I was forced not to say anything out, or I was dead meat at home!

Lastly, there was this one lady that would come to the house like every six months checking all the rooms and asking questions. Again, my mother would act as the holy Virgin Mary, knowing good and well she just murdered me the day before because I forgot to wash one dish in the sink! My father was usually at work at these times so she would be alone to deal with the lady. Now, this must have been the weed my mother was on one day after the lady left because evidently, there were rumors around the hood that people were getting paid monthly if their kids were too bad and hard to handle.

All you had to do was try them at the crazy house, and they will start cutting you a check. Can you believe my mother took me up there with confidence? Then afterward as we were on the way home, she told me while puffing her cig that she tried to get that check for me because I was off in the head and bad as hell. Another painful verbal hit but I was used to that already. I still had that lady on my mind from earlier though. Just all confusing and weird, yet I could never question my mother about it or that would land her big hand on my face until it swells.

So, who is it that I could talk to and get answers at such a young age? Then a light bulb pops in my mind after numerous times of thinking; I came up with an answer! Grandma Helen would surely tell me what was going on and she could answer the questions I had for her now that I've gotten older. Honestly, I felt the age didn't matter because she would talk to Stacy and me like grownups anyway! So sure enough, as soon as I got the chance to go to the country, I was at my grandma's neck with a thousand questions!

I knew that I didn't have much time, so I had to get it out of her quickly but she acted like she could not comprehend. Well, that became more confusing to me because she was like the walking tape recorder with me and now, someone pressed the stop button on her. Finally, I just gave up of course. My grandma told me that she wanted to see me more, but if she was going to be able to, she would have to be a little careful with her mouth. I could comprehend so I understood that a little I guess.

Well, as I started to reach the age of ten, another chapter in my life started to unfold. My mindset turned into jello just wandering all over the place and my insides had become so full of questions and pain all at once that it changed me tremendously. I started to become what I was going through, what I was around, what I was feeling, and what I was thinking. I started to learn and feel what anger meant, why I was crying 80 percent of the time even at school, what a good conscience and bad conscience was, and the feeling of being alone. Not to say it was intentional but it was time for a change with all this bottled in me.

Also being book-smart from my mother and street-smart hanging out with my father at the same time made it all that much better for this change in me. Studying what goes on at all times, being around more adults than children, around more street dudes than my own family, etc. Getting advice from my neighbors rather than a teacher at school or my parents who seemed to be lost in space. I had now realized that I'm alone with zero attention, but I was now guaranteed to get it. An entire new kid was forming into a product of what was going on in him and around him.

CHAPTER 5

PRODUCT OF MY ENVIRONMENT

"I don't want to be a product of my environment. I want my environment to be a product of me!"
-Jack Nicholson

"Be sure to do all of your homework guys and behave as you all go to the cafeteria for lunch today!" Ms. Edwards shouted to the classroom. As I sat there tuning her out, I would stare at the clock as it was slowly getting close to lunchtime. I was about half-past starving when the bell finally rang and as I walked out of the class, Ms. Edwards looked at me with a serious face saying, "Joshua, now you know you can do a lot better than what you are doing! You're such a smart kid; I would just hate to see it all go to waste baby!"

All I would do is reply an unbothered ok and keep it moving. You see, she had no idea what I was going through away from school and to me, I had bigger problems than a grade at school. I was so hungry as I sat down to finally eat my food that someone would offer me some of theirs because they must've felt my pain. Well, at least one person physically felt my pain. As I got to finish my food, some not so smart person decides to pick on me by putting their hand in my plate to take my biscuit!

I quickly grabbed his hand, bit his finger, and slapped him as hard as I could across his bottom jaw! Now you talk about a quick reflex! I was usually the one crying because of my confusing life but not this time buddy. He cried right on to the teacher that was on cafeteria duty which caused me to have another principal visit. Yes, I was pretty known at this point in the office after doing something out of the way numerous times. The most common would be throwing a temper tantrum at a teacher or just slapping a student.

I had begun to change for the worst and I didn't care at all. My mother never showed up at the schoolhouse and my father kind of slowed down at this point, seeing that we had even more things going against us at home. Our lights would be shut off occasionally months at a time, the bills were through the roof, and my parents would fight verbally and physically weekly! So for them, paying attention to what I had going on was the last thing on their mind. It was so bad at one time that the school would call home for my parents, but they weren't ever at home, so I would rush home and delete the messages as if nothing happened!

I was smart for all the wrong reasons at the time, which would come back to haunt me. The school I attended was very ghetto so, the teachers would wound up leaving it alone and just referring me to my school counselor, "Ms. Lady." I started to tell her a little too much now that I was older. I still abided by my parent's code, always to keep things silent, but the way I told her things she still wound up putting my words together. I'm a young kid that realizes that this lady is all I have to talk to in my life that will listen to me.

My father always said I should come to him for anything bothering me, but due to the circumstances at home, I think any kid would pass! My mother, on the other hand, thought she knew everything, she was never wrong, and was always negative so I wasn't going to her either. Well, I think I use to talk a little too much to the lady; I told her I was hungry a lot, I hated school, and best of all, I didn't want to go home. Now when that was said, she would freeze up and ask me why but, I never told.

It was like clockwork now with expensive looking people stopping by the house, sessions beefing up after school with counseling and court dates! Well, although this was all weird after talking to her once, the court dates was another story to tell. For instance, one day in the classroom I guess I had aggravated Ms. Edwards so badly, that she stood in front of the classroom and humiliated me fully saying, "I have an announcement to make class, so pay close attention. We have a student here in the class that is a very bad influence with all the potential in the world but will not use any of it. He can't keep his hands to himself, his grades are low, and he ignores me when I talk to him! Beware of Joshua Jackson's influence bringing you all down!"

These days you wouldn't be able to get away with saying things like that about a student, but back then this was normal. My feelings had dropped to the floor and before I could catch myself, I flipped the desk over and to the top of my lungs I screamed out, "F*** You Bi***!!!" Guys, before I knew it, she burst out into tears and while she cried, I took myself to the office because I knew what time it was. All I could think of was the pain I felt when she sounded like my mother for one whole minute in front of everyone in the class. She couldn't even make it to the principal's office. So she sent the next door teacher over on her behalf.

This time, the consequences were not good on my part and I couldn't take this one back. The principal suspended me until further notice or until both parents showed up to the school! Later that day, I saw Ms. Edwards as I loaded unto the bus huddled up with other teachers, I guess telling them what happened. I looked away as I slowly walked to the back of the bus in my spot looking out of the window with one tear dropping after another. I knew I was dead after my mother found this out and there was nothing I could do about it.

Then again, as I thought about it, a light bulb popped in my head with an idea thinking, "What if I get up early every morning and fake like I'm going to school but really I'm not? I'll just hide somewhere for eight hours straight?" Well people, that's exactly what I did for the next three days! Now understand that today, you can't do these types of things because of school laws, but I had it all planned out. I didn't tell my parents anything about being suspended and the school hadn't called so I thought my plan just might work. I woke up that morning, put my clothes on, stole some bologna out of the fridge, and off I was to the bus stop.

The plan was off to a great start because my nosey neighbors weren't out at all, due to probably being locked up in jail as normal and they would have had my back anyways. When I got to the bus stop, the kids that paid attention to me, I looked at them as mean as I could and told them, "If anybody tells that I didn't get on the bus, I'll kill you!" I never talked, I always looked mean; especially when word got around about me at school that I was the problem child. So, sure enough, I had no problems with them saying anything and it's crazy because the bus driver didn't even have a clue.

When I got through warning them, I would hide behind a huge tree as they all loaded the bus and wait for it to pull off. As the bus pulled off and got far enough ahead, I ran as fast as I could behind the houses in the hood so that no one could spot me not getting on the bus. There was an abandoned house not too far from my house and the bus stop, so I would sit in the back of it for the entire eight hour period! Talk about some crazy thinking for my age, just to keep from letting my parents know. I would sit there being bitten by mosquitoes, no lunch; just listening to the sirens that passed by.

I succeeded with this master plan for three whole days with a watch on my hand. I would listen to the sound of the bus loudly stopping, run to it and walk home with the other kids and some of the kids didn't even notice me. I got all the way to Wednesday perfectly until this time; it was just impossible to do. As I walk from behind the abandoned house, three of the noisiest ladies on earth were peeking at me talking amongst each other wondering what was going on with me.

Meanwhile, my father, out of all the times in the world decided to come home early and make the flower bed! My heartbeat was rushing as I tried to figure my way out of this, but it was impossible. My father could see from our raggedy house, all the way to the bus stop and the ladies were staring at me like a pack of wolves! Finally, they screamed at the top of their lungs at my father as I tried to run out another way, but it was too late. I was caught red-handed amid my master plan, only to have the worst to come out of this.

I looked back at the ladies with a sad glimpse as my father grabbed me by the arm verbally getting on to me, lost at what was going on. So before I could even enlighten him on what was going on, he called the school and they let him talk to Ms. Edwards personally! I knew I was dead, but something deep in me didn't care at the same time. When she got through telling my father everything, how long I was suspended, and the only way I could come back to school made life even tougher for me. My father knew he had to tell my mother and that she never goes to my schoolhouse. I also noticed that I wasn't so smart after all seeing that I couldn't go back to school anyway until they both showed up!

I think he was so mad at me that I didn't even catch a beating from him or my mother, at least not yet. Well, they set up the conference for early that next morning and boy was I in for a treat. You see, the principal didn't want to see my parents just for that one incident, they wanted to talk about every incident that happened. As we all sat in the office together, my mother looked at me like a red nose pit ready to lock onto me for dear life. I thought she was mad already, but that wasn't the half of my problems.

What I didn't share with them besides my behavior, was my backpack full of report cards with my horrible grades and my excessive skipping class! My grades were horrible and sometimes I just didn't feel like going to class. So I would stay in the bathroom away from everyone! Now, there was one person I had befriended due to my switching process from bad to terrible. His name was Martin, my next door neighbor and my principal sat there and told my parents all about him. How Martin was the one that supposedly gave me all of my influence and that we did some of the same things in school, including skipping and report card withholding.

My parents turned from black to red while they listened as I slowly pulled everything out of my backpack and laid it all on the table. Not only did it get me in trouble, but it also got them in bigger trouble because it was as if they were neglecting me period! They had no idea with what was going on with me, my next door neighbor, and on top of that, the school counselor had a feeling I was going through a lot as well. After all the talk was done and I apologized to Ms. Edwards, the ride home was silent as ever with long faces and lips poked out. When I got home, I was told to take everything off except my underwear and go outside as my mother cursed me out.

My father whipped me into a pulp in front of the whole neighborhood and my mother stood there cheerleading him on. At the same time, Martin's father was whipping his butt naked! Wow, word traveled really fast in our hood! As my Mother stood there, a woman across the street was yelling back and forth at her about child abuse and the police would be called on both my parents and Martin's. My mother didn't budge at all and sure enough, the police showed up and my parents turned into robots of perfection. This particular event in my life will never be forgotten because that day, things would open my mind up differently.

Shortly after the police came and left, the "expensive" people showed up again. This time they had questions galore, pictures taken of me naked, and court dates set due to this incident. They didn't take me away with them, but I wasn't slow and I felt like I was their product. As I finally sat alone in my room, I could hear the sounds of my mother yelling and bickering about me negatively while my blisters swell up on my body quickly. That day, I didn't know what death was fully, but I sure wouldn't mind trying it out. I didn't want to live anymore. No matter what Joshua had done – good or bad – It was always the wrong thing with the wrong results against me every time.

This one incident though can teach others that it is always very important to pay attention to your children at all times because things can get out of hand really quickly! Later that night, I had a soft knock on my slide window, it was Martin saying, "Wasssammm JJ, say look, I won't be taking any more beatings like that again, man I'm leaving and you should come with me ya heard me!" As I looked at him, I was scared because I didn't understand what he was saying. I felt my wounds throbbing and stinging at the same time, so I replied, "Let's do it bro!" Like the rookie I was, I left late that night with my only friend with not a bit of clothing, food to eat, or place to go!

We were two young kids from the same hood trying to find our young blind way. So, we took the walkway down the canal seeing that it ran a long way. Martin was older than me by a year, so I kind of looked up to him and followed his lead. As he was rushing me to walk faster, I stopped slowly when my nose caught the weirdest smell I'd ever known and Martin said, "OH, that's probably just the dumpster right next to you bro so let's keep moving before we get caught!" Before I could move any further toward him, I walked slowly closer to the dumpster and I almost screamed at the top of my lungs blurting out, "M, that's someone's arm man isn't it?" Martin came up behind me and slowly moved the cardboard and sheets that covered it. His eyes had gotten buck and he shouted, "JJ it's a dead body outche!"

He didn't have to tell me twice because before he finished his sentence, I was running as fast as I could the opposite direction as he got burned following behind! We made it a couple of blocks away from the body. As I caught my breath, I glanced at M and said, "Man I can't do this, I promise I won't tell nobody because that's how my mother raised me but, I'm going back home before we end up like that!" "Look JJ, we can't turn back now cuz if we do, we gonna end up like that with our parents, you can go back but I ain't!"

Martin said breathing heavily. I dapped him off and within an hour, I made it back home safely. Little did I know to make a long story short guys that it would be the last time I would see Martin. In fact, the next day since it was the weekend, his parents knocked on our door and asked if we had seen him. My parents had no idea that I had tried to run away with him last night. So I sat in the back room as always and didn't speak a word! I was worried about him because he was the only friend I had; we were in a similar situation and someone was dead last night.

I'm barely ten years old and I've seen so much from crackheads, drugs, violence, women my father had, and my second dead body. I knew the killings were bad in our area but to see one in person close up was amazing. I was also afraid for him because in our whole parish, babies and kids got shot up every day like it was a hobby and we would all hear about it in school. Months would pass by and still no Martin at all. Of course, I didn't get out much, so I didn't know if there might have been a search going on or if they have found him. It was even weirder when his parents wound up moving away and some new people moved in with two daughters soon after they left.

So that became the end of the Martin saga for me. He would be the first friend I lost early in my life. Meanwhile, fast-forwarding time, the lights are back off at the house, and the rats were having a party in the walls while I was getting ready for my new school, New Year, but same testimonies. Sad to say that I can't remember what school I attended, but I know it was located not too far from the Fischer Projects where we also use to live. I think it was William J. Fischer. As I arrived at the school, I saw all the kids wearing starter jackets with their favorite football teams on them, fresh Nike or Reebok shoes, and top brand clothing.

There I was standing with the shoes I wore last year from KMart, clothes picked out by my mother, and the look on my face was like here we go again. After what had happened to my friend, I decided to stay distant even more from people. This school year, I wanted to work on myself but trouble seems to always follow when you're a product of what you've been going through. I had four different teachers and not a whole two weeks passed me by before I got put out of one of their classes – Ms. Franklinton's class. She was actually my favorite teacher, beautiful as ever and was pregnant. Someone was picking on my shoes, so I flipped them over in their desk shortly after.

I must've told Ms. Frank I was sorry twenty times. I didn't want the same problems as last year and I began to teach myself the art of never getting caught again. She wound up letting me slide and it wasn't her first time. It's as if this particular teacher felt my pain and felt sorry for me at times, but soon my luck would run out in the year. I was still going through a lot back at home. For instance, we had finally gotten put out of the house we were living in and was forced to move into a roach motel. My parents couldn't afford it anymore due to some bad life choices.

Well, the motel decision was worse than the house because my mother DID NOT LIKE THAT AT ALL, so god help me. First off, she had to start coming to pick me up from school every day when it was over and that was not her cup of tea. Now, she didn't come in but she would pull up late for me outside. Secondly, she acted like I was contagious not wanting me to take a bath in the same tub they took theirs, always speaking about privacy. Lastly, I was forced to do my homework and once I was finished, I had to turn my head the opposite way of the television. As cartoons like Darkwing Duck and Goofy played in the background every day, I would cry myself to sleep, wondering why my father won't grow some nuts and finally do something about this. Nothing changed and this routine went on as long as we lived there next to being homeless. Instead of going through that, I sure wouldn't have minded going back to the rats on Huntsville Street and shelter myself in my room.

My father and I would still be doing yard work for his extra money, pleasure, and my mother was still at the slot machines complaining about her life. So, by the time I got to school after going through these things at home, I'll be exhausted. I got to Ms. Franklinton's class one day and she has a task for me to do so she said, "Joshua, you are a very bright kid and two of your stronger subjects are English and math. When you get home, I want you to tell your parents to help you start counting money. I see you are very good with numbers in your head, but practice counting money now!"

I gave her a big smile and nodded my head. This beautiful black woman had no idea I didn't even have a home. I still ran and told my mother all the good stuff Ms. Frank said but she just barely smiled at me and referred me to my father being that he's the one that knows math very well. That was a very bad decision. My mother wound up having to go to work so my father was there with me and I know she delivered the message to him so he said, "You see, I always said you were the king of the jungle son keep it up! Don't worry about mama, you know her and her family isn't affectionate at all, but it's ok.

Now she told me you need to know that math and I'm going to show you like I was raised!" My smile quickly went to a frown. I was excited my father complimented me unlike my mother, but I was terrified of what might happen next. My father was raised with beatings in some cases, and at this time, I could tell he was high off drugs! A smart kid I was because, after about ten minutes of me counting those coins and messing up, his patience went out the door. He grabbed a belt from the motel closet and he whipped my hand that I counted with. He would shout with force, "Don't nothing else matter if you can't count your money son now count that money right!"

My father didn't know all that I was going through, he rarely whipped me a lot, and he had a great heart, but he was just so blind to things like this. You don't whip your child to help them count money and especially when you're high under the influence. I tell you one thing though, after that incident I've been good with money ever since! When I went to school, I counted money to perfection but my hand was throbbing with a mind full of thoughts like, "I should stab him while he is asleep, tell my mother who he cheats with, start skipping school again, etc."

I held my composure though because I actually had events like this happen before with my mother. For instance, I would have to spell words for hours with her over and over again to perfection and reading would be no different. I would have to read books that were way ahead of my time with huge words. If I didn't pronounce one correctly or didn't finish reading in a certain time, I was whipped. I would have to stand up and hold the book with one hand in front of her as I was forced to make hand gestures like a young speaker. "You gonna work to be that king your daddy always talking about and everything you do gonna be different than others," she replied.

She meant just what she said because I got whipped for slipping up on any of it. She would always tell me that white folks always gonna be better, but I have the chance to be just like them if not better. She was always negative while I was growing up, but I also learned to look at a few things as positive to help me become even smarter. So back at school, I began to receive awards of mastery and overachievement being the top in reading and writing but coming second to one girl I had the dearest crush on named Brooke. That crush didn't last long because she was killed in a drive-by shooting shortly after I had become close to her.

This life around us had also become normal due to different hoods beefing with one another. Going forward, just another environmental issue that started in our school. You see these hoods I speak about were ran by Original Gangsters better known as OGs but they also had children that attended my school. These children were the new generation of gangsters turning the schoolhouse into a street zoo. This was already my cup of tea because I already had a history of wrongdoings. This would become a new level though. I was older, smarter, and tired of not having family or friends. So, I joined one of the crews easily! Led by an older kid that had been held back in school twice already because of his grades. He was the shortest in the crew but he was ruthless.

I was a car rider at the time, so my mother used to drop me off at the top of my rode when I got out of school so that I could walk home while she headed off somewhere and I was alone as usual. Well, on this particular day, as I was walking home, I saw him and his mother arguing about something. Guys, next thing you know, I stared in amazement as his mother was walking him home holding him while yelling. He was punching her hard as he could in her face numerous times with his right hand as she held his left arm! You could hear the blows as she kept dragging him and continuously abusing his mother.

Everyone stood and watched not saying a word because they knew that his family wasn't nothing to mess with. When something came down to him or his family, no one ever told or called the police. If I did that to my mother, I would be dead! Now, his mother did call herself snatching him up a little but THAT wasn't enough. His right arm would not stop swinging at her, and his mouth blurted out curse words while doing so. By the way, everyone called him Little G or just G. I guess that was short for little gangster. All I know is that I had never and until this day have never seen any kid do that to their mother before!

Well, G stayed on the next block over from me so by the time I made it close to home, they disappeared out of sight. Yes, we had gotten another place to stay that was even worse than the hotel, and still a one bedroom full of roaches. I slept in the front room on the floor while my parents took the bedroom. Anyways, I don't know what happened to G at home that night, but the next morning, he was the same as if nothing happened. When I got dropped off to school the next morning, he was there acting a clown in the cafeteria.

"Wassup JJ! Ya momma still got you coming around us with them payless shoes on huh?" He asked as he talked to me with an evil grin. He continued, "Today, ima show you how to cop some fresh ones and we ain't even gotta pay ya heard me!" I looked at him shyly nodding my head asking him, "What I gotta do though?" "I got you fool, just meet me after the bell rings at the water fountain outside!" He replied still grinning. As always, I nodded my head and I was outside at the fountain soon after the bell rung. The other kids were in class but I and G were doing exactly what I was afraid of falling into again, skipping class! He said he liked me because I was solid, always quiet, and I ain't with the snitching!

I would have loved to have a big brother instead of being alone. I guess since Martin was gone here we go again with G. I had hung out with G and his crew many times but this event I'm about to tell you stood out more. As we left the water fountain, this guy picked us up in a black cutlass with nice rims on it. It was G's older cousin taking us to wherever G wanted to go. I loved cars at the time because I had so many toy cars in the toy box I use to play with before we started moving from place to place.

It was around the year 1995 during school hours and here we are, riding around in the hood until suddenly the car stops and we all hopped out. G tells his cousin that lil JJ really needs some shoes so let's hit these niggas up. The car was never shut off and here's why. Before I knew it, G and his cousin were forcing me to take some Nikes off of an innocent teenager in his early 20s black guy walking the street. G stood about 5 foot 5 but had hands of lighting, hitting the guy while his cousin held a big black gun to the guy's head holding him, while I snatched his shoes.

I finally got the shoes off, ran to the car as G jumps in, the cousin still points the gun as he gets in, and pulls off like a NASCAR driver. We make like twenty different turns before we finally slowed down and everyone busts out laughing. "We got that nigga cuz for real!" G said with his little voice. His cousin parked the car and said, "Man we got that nigga's watch, his money, and his shoes!" "You did good lil JJ, no lie ya heard me you the truth!" Till this day, I remember those exact words from his cousin. I had never once heard my mother say anything like that to me before and my father would commend me on things all the time but his actions showed something different so, I was convinced this was my real family.

With the money he'd stolen, guys I even ate my first piece of seafood that we stopped and bought somewhere in the hood. My mother always said that seafood or any high price meat was not for children at all and that I'm only allowed to eat bologna. G and his cousin, got some of my stories that day as we rode around the city like New Orleans youngest convicts, skipping school. I wasn't afraid anymore around them and nor was I shy so we talked a lot. G's mother was a crackhead, and at this time, I learned that cocaine and pills were heavily used and sold.

I guess that explains him beating her and on my side, my father's addiction. Going forward in my story, we would do this skipping routine often, learning the school systems, attendance rules, G's family member serving the principal the same thing my parents were smoking, and I even learned how to start a vehicle without the keys. You see, life had gotten so tough and overwhelming for my parents that it was back to square one with them not paying attention to me again.

I studied their schedules nonstop although, certain things would be tough for me to do seeing that I lived in the small living room of a one bedroom apartment on the floor. Of course, I would eventually get caught as always but this particular time, was a turning point and here's why. My mother was off to work one morning while my father actually stayed home for a change. Now, at the time my father had been staying away from home for long periods of time like when I was younger but this particular time he stayed so I studied the situation wrongly!

As you know, I usually get taken to school but this time we had begun to have bus service in the area, so my parents were informed. Well, I pulled another one of my stunts again, and of course, I didn't get onto the bus. I went to G's house looking for him only to find out from his family that his cousin had been shot and killed in the same car we use to ride in! Also, the police raided G's house, arrested a few people, took his mother, and he went to Jefferson Parish juvenile center! This situation was all a mess and I was lost on what it all meant guys but I had learned a lot from G and his family.

I had received all of this info from his uncle which was his next door neighbor that was totally different and had no dealings with that life asking me, "Why ain't you in school young man? You know the police and the child protective services cracking down on all that so be careful; don't end up like my family boy, now go!" He didn't have to tell me twice as I zipped through the hood running like crazy but it was too late. Before I could get far enough away from his house, two police cars were behind me. All I could think about was everything he just told me added to everything else I was dealing with at home. "What if I go to a kid's jail? What are the Child Protective Services? What is Juvenile Center? What if I get beat outside again? What if the place they take me to is worse than where I stay now?" I asked myself quickly in my mind. Well, those questions suddenly turned into one answer as they turned their sirens on my mind said, "RUN!"

I ran like never before and the two cop cars chased behind me! It was as if I was in a famous action movie at only ten years old. I climbed fences, jumped, ran, hid, and started running again when, of course, I ran into some cops that were on feet. The chase was over, but the fun had just begun. As they breathed heavily, they asked me aggressively why I was running, why I wasn't in school, and where my parents were. No response was my middle name and I wasn't about to tell on myself for nothing so, I stayed quiet until they ask me the third time where my parents were.

"They're both at work right now, and I was late for the school bus, just trying to get a ride, sir," I replied as if I was being smart only to dig myself a deeper hole. "Well I tell you what, we're going to go ahead and cuff you up, put you in the car, take you down to the station, but before that, we're going to nail a little letter on your apartment door telling them we got you ok?" The officer said while putting me in the car slowly and breathing heavily. I was in full shock, handcuffed in the back of a police car and all I could think about was "please daddy when they nail this letter, DO NOT wake up!"

Sure enough, we got to my house, nailed the letter, and my father opened the door slowly with big eyes saying, "Josh? Wait, what's going on?" "Well Mr. Jackson, we were just getting ready to take your son down to the station because he said you weren't home and he missed the school bus this morning. Mr. Jackson, I don't have to tell you that this type of behavior could put you all in a lot of trouble, and judging on his running this morning, he looks skilled at this, not to mention him being sighted at a drug house we raided! Now, I'm going to be straightforward with you that we're going to have to report this to CPS and put your son in our system.

What we won't do is charge anyone today, but you may be getting a phone call or a visit soon for neglecting. As for you Joshua, stay in school and run at recess, not from the police!" The officer replied as he took the cuffs off of my little hands. He also told us to be careful due to a big storm coming our way, which would flood our area as always. I don't know if it was god, my father being high or just scared out of his mind, but I didn't receive a beating this time. Even when my mother made it home, I got cursed out and starved for the night but there was still something different in the air.

My parents weren't even talking at the time and like I had said before, my father was barely home. His rendezvous was catching up with him and my mother was starting to get fed up more than ever. Well, with another friend in my life gone now, my parents going through it, me acting like a project product, and to top it off "Expensive people" snooping around our doorstep more than usual, life was about to change for the worse in a brand new chapter people! This time changing our lives. Shall we?

CHAPTER 6

LIFE CHANGING LEGAL CHALLENGES

"Challenges are what make life interesting and overcoming them is what makes life meaningful!"
-Joshua J. Marine

"As the night cries tears of rain, I cry tears of pain. Am I the one to blame or for me do they feel ashamed. Scars on my legs, my back, and my hands for beatings I can't explain. For the children, I know their lives and their thoughts are not the same. They call their rooms their own to stay. Mommy calls this room I'm in just somewhere to lay. Never a smile on her face. In the ghetto with the "other ladies" is where my daddy lay. Gunshot bullets sounding like whistles, unanswered bodies I've seen at an early age. My friends are lost, with no family to gain. All by myself, as the night cries tears of rain, I cry tears of pain."

It was 1996-97 at eleven to twelve years of age and here I am writing one of many poetic thoughts down on paper while it was dark and raining outside. You see, writing was the thing for me to do at that time because I didn't have what the other kids had. Writing and reading was my getaway from, and listener to my thoughts. My mother would read some of my poems saying she didn't understand them and, she wouldn't even compliment me. My father never knew I was writing, even though he was the parent attending my school occasionally.

They even gave him an award for doing so, at one time but he still didn't see me as he should have. Well, one night as I was trying to sleep, I heard my mother crying and screaming at the top of her lungs cursing vigorously saying, "I'm so tired of his shit! He can have them whores he dealing with because I am done with this!" As I crawled under the sofa, I could hear a tsunami taking place in their room. A storm full of flying objects thrown by my mother, broken glasses, and a mouth full of screams taking place. It had happened before but this was by far one of the worst incidents.

I guess she had found out about another woman because as usual, my father hadn't been home in a couple of days in this roach infested one bedroom. As I laid there on the floor until morning, not once did she come to check on me at all. Somehow, I fell asleep for a couple of hours and was awoken by the pitbulls barking next door. While the sunlight shined inside the house, I slowly came from under the sofa and went straight to the door. I peeked into their room, and my mother was gone without telling me anything.

Glass was everywhere; pictures were broken, the bed was flipped, the T.V. was busted up, the smell of bleach was lurking from clothes on the floor, and the list goes on. It was a school day so I had to rush and get ready. I tiptoed over the mess in the house and off I was to school. I had to catch a ride with my neighbor; his name was Joshua as well. This particular day, we got dropped off at the store right down from the school because I told them I would like to walk the rest of the way so, Joshua wound up getting out with me. His mother looked at us and told us to be careful.

As we walk to the store, I glanced at Joshua and said, "Hey Josh; ima go in the store real quick man I'm kind of hungry you want something?" He replied, "I'm ok JJ, I'll wait outside." I nodded my head and I went inside with so much on my mind you wouldn't even imagine at this age. I remember like yesterday grabbing a bag of Elmer's, Zapps chips, and a Neehi cold drink. I slowly look up at the Chinese at the register, with people in line paying no attention to me, I did the worst thing ever.

With no money in my hand to pay, I jetted out of the store in a coincidence to see two cops pulling up, Josh halfway up the damn street, and the Chinese owner pointing at me saying, "Hey! He stole from me!" My heart was racing as the police stopped me in my tracks and I had nowhere to run! Here I was, after a night full of my mother going nuts, me not knowing if my father was ok, and a handful of items I hadn't paid for, getting ready to be handcuffed once again.

As they put the cuffs on me and got ready to take me downtown, a guy pulled up and said, "Hey y'all, please let him go that's my nephew and I'll deal with him accordingly, I promise you so take this money hea!" As I looked up at his face, I had recognized who he was. He was from Kenner in Susan Park where I used to live and he knew everything that went on in the hood. Everyone called him "Big Unc" because he was like that uncle that always tried to encourage you to be better growing up. Well, it seemed as if the officers knew him well themselves so in amazement they let me go free and Unc paid for my stuff, and we were off on our way.

"Boy you out here again doing this nonsense I've talked to you about before! Where your mama nem at?" he asked abruptly. I replied, "I'm sorry Unc, I was just hungry and my mama nem I don't know where they at, ya heard me. They weren't at home when I left, and I think my mama was hurt for something my dad did last night but it's none of my business." So, Unc sat back in his sit and replied, "JJ, I want you to listen to me boy. I know you been going through stuff that these other little kids running around here don't go through, I know all about GG, I know all about Martin and your parents. You are a strong young boy and you've been smart ever since you were a little bitty something, catching the school bus by yourself.

Nephew, you have got to be better than your surroundings and understand that you can be great! Stealing, skipping school, and hanging with these boys around here ain't gonna get you nowhere but dead or in jail before you become a teenager! Now, I'm going to drop you off at school but nephew always remember what I've told you nah, I'm serious ya heard!? What are you doing living out here anyway boy? This here worse than where you started! Just try to be positive though, and if you ever need me you know where I stay and remember what I say in case we never meet again, now go boy on you late!"

I got out of the car running towards the school, and I slowly stopped to turn and look back at Unc. He looked at me pointing his finger and I turned back around to continue my way in! I was late for school again with nobody to check me in. This was a big problem. I was allowed to stay at school the rest of the day though and to my surprise, my mother was waiting for me outside with the rest of the car riders. I jumped in the car as she said hey, I responded saying hey as well, with nothing else being said the whole way home.

I didn't ask what was going on and she didn't give me any explanation on the situation either. As we arrived home, I noticed a lady was there waiting for us. At this point, I had an idea of who she was and why she was there. "Excuse me Ms. Jackson, your son was caught trying to steal this morning on the way to school but the officers let him go due to his Uncle." My mother replied with shocked, "I had no idea about this and who is your uncle boy?" I had no response as I dropped my head. "Also, Ms. Jackson, there have been reports of Joshua being late for school, not showing up, and low satisfactory grades.

As I look around in this neighborhood, I'm also frightened myself of the environment he is living in. Is everything alright here at home Joshua?" She asked. I nodded my head but my god, my mother went into a frenzy saying, "Now you listen to me lady! We are doing everything we can for our son and he is doing just fine! Please do not judge us as parents by the environment we live in or what you think is going on because you have no idea! As for his schooling, he will do better and we will work on that with him more, but no one will take my son!" The lady paused, glanced at me, glanced at my mother, and said slowly, "Ms. Jackson, I'm afraid we're going to have to discuss these matters in court in front of the judge. I am very sorry but in our files, it shows these incidents and actions have become occasional. Meanwhile, if I were you, I would do my best to keep Joshua out of any more trouble, love him hard, and get as far away from here as you can!

The way things are looking, he'll be in juvenile detention or coming back with me in no time and that is definitely not what you want! Think about what I said Ms. Jackson and we'll be in touch." As the lady drove off, my mother started crying as she walked inside and slowly shut the door to her room. I sat down on the floor of the front looking up at the ceiling, just thinking of what kind of beating I would get this time. Hours would pass by that day, my mother would never come out from the room and my father never showed up.

I just laid there thinking about all the events that happened that day, from waking up to a trashed house, getting saved by Unc, and getting a set of court dates by some expensive looking lady. You see, one thing the reader will notice about my book is that the early stages of Joshua are so much to take in for a child that it's amazing. For instance, my mother finally came out from the room about 2 am. You would think things would have died down by now, but oh no, things just got a little worse.

At this point, I've learned that my mother was getting tired of me period; but even more tired of my father. He hasn't been home in a couple of days and she is infuriated. She paced back and forth and in and out of the apartment so much that you knew something bad was going to happen. As she smoked cig after cig, walking back and forth she was mumbling, "I swear if he shows back up tonight, I will kill him! I'm so sick and tired of this man I'm going to kill him! God I'm going to get rid of him!" All I remember doing was watching her as I sat far back from her cursing and pacing in the front room.

Suddenly, she stopped in their room though and didn't come out again. I started getting nervous due to the quietness, the low mumbling and a large set of clicking sounds. I decided to slowly go peak at what my mother was doing or at least hear what she was saying while the door was opened. As I look into their room slowly, I was shocked, still standing in the middle of the doorway as if I had seen a real ghost! I witnessed my mother loading bullets in a small chrome and white gun. As she quickly tried to cover it up from me seeing it, tears rolled down my eyes as she shouts, "Boy get your f***ing ass out of here right now, before I put you out in the street!

I can't stand either one of y'all asses, and your daddy better pray he doesn't come home tonight!" Well, just as well as she was sarcastically praying, I was seriously hoping he didn't come. My childhood life was built on pain and challenges that I had no answers to but, now this. If my father walked through that door, he would have been dead. I knew judging from the way she treated me that she would have no problem pulling the trigger! As the morning approached, I still hadn't slept and my mother was still awake as well, residing outside smoking cigarettes back to back.

Finally, after a few hours, she came inside and the lights were out. It seemed as if the minute she laid down though, the door opened and the lights came back on. It was my father dirty from head to toe full of oil, gas, and dirt! I immediately ran and hugged him because I didn't have a television to watch but I did know from a few movies that people hug before they die. In other words, I just knew this was my father's last day. I cried once again, as I pulled the covers over my head on the floor, and peeked out to get a front room view of what was going to take place. He called my mother in the front room and he wasted no time explaining himself.

I actually got to see my father in action and the way he can turn things around with his gift of gab, talking his way out of things. I actually can't remember all he said but I do know whatever he said, it worked and my mother never pulled out the gun. He was still punished and put in the front with me as he slept on the couch; I slept on the floor as always. For a while, my father had seemed to be behaving and I was the one still having trouble in school. In the back of my mind, I had images and quotes of Unc to keep with me when it came to doing certain things going forward.

There is a saying today that I didn't know as a kid though, "Trouble always seems to find those who run away from it!" Must've been true for me because my doings created consequences for us called court dates. Whether I had run away from home, been handcuffed, slapped a kid, or cursed out my teacher, I was held accountable for it and put in the system. It all confused me because no other kids I knew had to deal with this. They were disciplined by their parents and the rest would be history of growing up. As for me on the other hand, I was always getting house visits from people taking pictures of me naked with odd questions, after school doctors for questioning, and school counselors such as "Ms. Lady."

Although confused, I had no choice but to stand in front of the judge and tell the truth about things I was asked right? That's a negative! I was solid, telling the judge nothing personal about me. Until the next and final court date in the city of New Orleans, I grew tired of lying! I was sleeping on the floor of a roach-infested apartment, my childhood was absent due to numerous work by my father, and I was treated like dirt by my mother! I was a cry baby due to these events of losing my friends and never being held or told I love you. I had become a product at an early age and by the looks of things these people in the courthouse had other plans for me, besides going back home.

As I stood in front of the judge this time accompanied by my mother, the judge asked that I position the mike in front of my mouth and speak clearly. This time was different. He shifted the conversation towards me a whole lot more asking me, "Joshua, are you happy? Do you think your education is important? Do you think you hurt your parents when you do bad things? Do you believe you can be someone when you grow up?" The list goes on as if he was attacking me, but he suddenly asked me a question that had never been asked before, "Joshua, in your little world of trouble making, if you are scared of anyone or anything, who is it?" As I glanced at my mother, I looked back at the judge and replied, "My mommy.

I am scared of my mommy!" It was as if the courthouse went silent that instant as the words left my mouth. I could feel my mother breathing hot fire down the side of my neck she was standing on, as I wouldn't look her way after I said it. The judge continued and said, "Son, sometimes in life in order to make new changes, we need new situations. At the rate you are going, you're going to end up somewhere you don't want to be. You seem like a smart kid with a promising future but not in the city of New Orleans! This session is over, Ms. Jackson I would like to see you for a minute if you will." That's a day I would never forget, till this day of me writing my story because he was right.

When he said that, images popped in my head of my old friends, my old teacher Ms. Edwards and her negative words about me, and life that I had gone through before meeting the judge. I knew I would get consequences for what I said but I didn't care. All I cared about was hoping my parents would consider us leaving before either my father or me wound up somewhere bad. Well, sure enough, my mother got in the car, turned around in the back seat and slapped me all in my face for what I said. I cried on the way home and took the curse words that flew out of her mouth but I couldn't get this all off of my mind.

I had a high "dream filled" mind where I felt like day after day it would all get better, my parents will finally love me, and we would be a family. The legal hardships had just gotten worse for my family all thanks to my father. Guys, we just could not catch a break! But, before I explain my father's situation, there was something else that happened to me not too long after my final court date that my mother never exposed to my father. You guys remember when I got caught stealing and Unc saved me, my neighbor Josh ran before it happened right?

Well, I decided to steal his bike and take it for a ride. My mother with everything going on had prohibited me from leaving out of the yard but I left anyway strolling Josh's bike down the street. I ended up on a street where my mother had a girlfriend who she smoked weed with and she got her hair done. As I stroll down the street, I heard screams, everybody running, and loud gunshots!

As I got ready to try and turn around, I felt a hot burning sensation coming from my right shoulder bleeding slowly as I landed sideways on the ground! I screamed, using my left hand to hold my right arm as I could hear people yelling, "It's a kid! It's a kid! OMG!" It will seem unbelievable when I tell you guys who picked me up from the ground, as I screamed in excruciating pain! It was Unc once again as if he were my guardian angel! Unc DID NOT take me to a hospital; instead, he took me to an old lady's house that was full of incense burning, medicines, and tools as if she was some type of witch doctor. I was too young to know what was going on, who shot who, or who saw me. All I did know was that I was in pain and that this lady had to fix me! Unc was a lifesaver because Unc and the lady took care of me that day, in a hood way but my father would never know this incident happened.

I actually found out that I had been hit by a rebounding bullet that bounced off of something and ended up skipping my shoulder. As I laid there, she looked into my eyes differently from my mother and said to me, "You are a special child. Your arm will be just fine, as long as you keep it wrapped up and you do as I tell you. You are a young leader son and many great things are to come for you ok?" I nodded my head still in pain as I lay there thinking, "What does she mean?

My mother gonna kill me since the bullet didn't, and this is karma for leaving the yard and stealing a bike! Unc must have read my mind partially because he said that my mom's friend already knew what was up, so she told my mother that she would watch me while she took care of my father. Her friends knew how my mother treated me, so she knew I would be dead if I were to tell my mother the truth. So, I never did and as for my arm; if I could hide in the back of a house starving and getting eaten up by mosquitoes for 8 hours a day, then I think I could keep this from my mother who barely pays attention to me anyways.

Besides, this will eventually go away and it did just that as the days went by quickly at that. Whatever that lady put on me, it was working. As for Unc, he was like my guardian angel even though he didn't even stay in our hood. I didn't get it and I never will truthfully. The people that did the shooting bless their hearts, but this thing was nothing new in New Orleans. Well, this story just keeps getting better and better right? Not too long after this incident, life couldn't have gotten any worse because my father had messed up again so badly that it was said to have been on the news.

My mother went on a rampage and packed all of our things, this time to take me to one of the most hurtful places in life once again, and that was being homeless. She put all of our things in the car and she didn't give me a choice on whether I wanted to stay with my daddy or go with her. Here we are, me and my fed up mother, living in her car for days. I remember vividly like it was yesterday going to that same gambling donut shop taking "wash offs" in the bathroom sink for school smelling like yesterday. I would sleep in the car with the clothes covering the windows. I was already used to being the butt joke and getting picked on. This was one of the most crucial times in our lives at this point as my father kept doing things that I paid the consequences for. It was so bad at this point that I remember my mother calling my grandma Helen letting her know that we might be coming to live with her soon and that she couldn't take anymore.

I knew if Linda called Helen, life was really tough for us because they still didn't get along, so you could only imagine that. Now what's crazy is, I really did not know what happened but what I do know is that we wound up getting out of the living in the car situation and going back home. When we did so, I think it was in the hopes of patching things back up with her and my father. The truth is that my father was in jail and headed for about 20 years in prison for drugs. The kicker was that he got caught with another lady behind my mother's back in a car full of drugs in it.

The lady had been who he was dealing with for quite some time and they were into drugs together. Well, while he was in jail, a phone call was made to his mother Mildred Smith and got him released from jail, but check out what happens next. The following day after he was released, we were back at home now, so my father picked me up to hang out with him one last time before my mother takes me away for good as she claimed. As we were hanging out, he wasted no time in taking me straight to the dope-filled trap house full of junkies and crack sellers!

I sat on the hood of the car as I was told while he went inside as if he didn't just get out of jail awaiting his trial! God must have touched my father at the right time because something told him to make a store run real quickly. So he asked if anyone wanted to ride with him and I. Everyone decided to stay and get high while my father and I went around the corner to the store. Well, as we were coming back from the store, my father noticed a helicopter flying above with police coming from numerous directions at a time, headed the same way we were headed.

As we slowly crept around the corner, the crack house was surrounded by police and overhead was a helicopter! My father looked in astonishment as he quickly drove us far away from the place, scared to death. As we pulled up back home, my father started to cry, obviously overwhelmed with his addiction, his court case, and us leaving for good. Thank God we at least wouldn't be living in the car anymore since we were going to grandma house! As we headed down the causeway bridge, my mother called her aunt Janice to assist her once the trial starts for my father.

I wound up having to stay at my grandma's house alone while she was at work. My mother and my aunt pulled off on the way to see my father and his side chick in court. My father ended up beating all charges and granted a second chance and told to leave the city as advised by the judge. Imagine what would have happened if he was caught at the trap house. God had given him a chance of a lifetime instead of letting him get thrown away! That sounded very much similar to what the judge told me about leaving as well. With my mother and me living with my grandma and me not seeing my father at least sometimes, was a rough time for me.

Life around here was different from the New Orleans scene and it would take some time getting used to it. From running from police, being beaten, writing poetic stories, hiding behind houses, getting shaded by a bullet, being homeless, and many more experiences, I was now traumatized! I guess it was time to move on and create a new chapter the best way I could!

CHAPTER 7

A CHILD TRAUMATIZED

Definition: Subject to lasting shock as a result of an emotionally disturbing experience or physical energy!

Mark Goulston, a prominent psychiatrist wrote and I quote, "Trauma shatters your most basic assumptions about yourself and your world" -- "Life is good," "I'm safe," "People are kind," "I can trust others," "The future is likely to be good," -- and replaces them with the feelings like, "The world is dangerous," "I can't win," "I can't trust other people," and the list continues to go on!

At this point in my life, I had felt this way crying inside for help as I started my new life in Amite, Louisiana. The move was weird because as you all know, the relationship between my mother and grandma was terrible. Yaa, we had to start off living with my grandma until we got on our feet. You would think I would love it because when I was younger it was great, but this was the total opposite! The good thing was that it was right during the summer time so I had a break from school, and I could hang out with Stacy, Michael, and other kids on Bennett Rd.

Meanwhile, my father was still in New Orleans dealing with the fact that he didn't have my mother. Well, you all that have read my book from the beginning, understand that due to my mother's love for my father, the breakup didn't last long. My parents ended up getting back together after

Jehovah's witnesses, Mr. and Mrs. Quinn, counseled my father like they've always done – that I failed to mention to you guys.

Of course, he begged my mother to come back and she got tired of staying with my grandmother! So by the time summer ended, my father came back to the country for good this time and we got our own place to stay on James Rd. Now at the time, I was in a trauma state, after all, I had been through already, but in reality, I was still a kid so I did build a relationship with someone I would never forget and that was Michael Wilson. I spoke about him and his sister a little earlier in my book but he and Stacy didn't treat me any different because I was different from others.

I learned sports through him, his mother would cook for me like my grandma, and I would spend nights with his family. He was like a brother to me and to top it off; I learned that other kids went through life situations as well that I could relate to. Michael had a skin condition all over his body, and he took a lot of medicine but he smiled every day as if it did not bother him. He was great in sports and he had a close-knit family behind him. That was one summer, one friend, and one family, I'll never forget till this day! Now, I had other family members beside Stacy that have seen me, talked to me a little, and I visited their house occasionally but we could never hang out.

For instance, Elliot, Nae, Rob, Ben, and a few more. Ben's mama was friends with my grandma but he picked on me A LOT because he was ten times bigger than me! Rob, was the baby boy of Marcy that gave him anything he wanted, spoiling him so I definitely couldn't hang out with him. Personally, we've talked several times while we were younger but after being spoiled, he grew up to be something I didn't understand while still living with his mother. I mean, how can somebody claim to be from the streets, indulge in their type of activities and end having a great life?

I told the readers earlier that I studied people and I studied just good enough to stay my distance. Nae is my cousin and she picked on me just like Ben! Right now, I don't talk to her at all. Now Elliot was and still is the Bennet Roads big dog. The reason I say that is because he never had a hard life and everybody knew him. If there were a new video game or clothing to come out, he would have it. The tears that I shed and the tears that he shed were TOTALLY opposite. His mother and father stayed across from his grandmother. She stayed down from his great auntie and his great auntie down from one of her nieces.

I had never seen anything like this family closeness, especially next to one another. I guess it kind of reminded me of GG and his family. The weird part was that each one of them was relatives to my grandma but they weren't in contact a lot. Elliot had a younger brother Dre, who was just as spoiled. When they cried, I would watch in amazement as it would be something such as a game, something they wanted to do or be done for them. Now don't get me wrong, I admired the closeness of the family but the whining over things that some of us in the ghetto dreamed of was amazing to me. His mother, Jackie was a woman I dreamed of having as a mother! Now, although these were my cousins, they treated their outside friends better than me. I was nothing to them and the same goes for the way I started to feel about how my parents felt about me. At this point in my life, I was full of trauma but I was smart enough to know I was not their kinfolk. Of course, I know my mother had a lot to do with many people not wanting to deal with me on certain levels because they wanted nothing to do with her. This would work out for the best for me in the future, though because cousins like Elliot, would become just what I studied them to be further along in the story!

Ok so, let's get back to my father taking us from my grandmas to James Rd. So, my father beats his charges and I got a fresh start from all my pain, and my mother finally gets away from her mother into a country home away from trouble right? Well, not quite! You see, James Rd was one of the worst moves of our lives! I thought for sure that I would still have to put up with a little pain from my mother, that ghetto life was behind us, and my father has changed his life. Well, my thoughts were wrong, as we pulled up to our shack of a home that my parents will be paying rent for.

The shack looked like one of the trap houses that my father and I used to be at. As I stood back observing in amazement of what we were getting ready to live in, my father gave his speech, "Now you guys, the owner said it might take some time to get a toilet in here and the ceilings fixed. We've already been through a lot, so God is going to get us through this ok. We have nowhere to go, so let's make this a home. Son, for now we're going to be using the bathroom in these buckets for the time being because we don't have a toilet. You and I, will take them out to the back, dump them, and bring them back in, to be reused.»

My heart stopped and my ears shut admittedly from hearing anything else he had to say. All I could imagine at that moment was, "Who takes a dump in a bucket as if this was a history book story? God, why do I have to be the one to dump the buckets? I'm being punished all over again in the country now, damn!" As we got settled in the house finally, I remembered my father did speak more about putting pots down for the ceiling leaks until they were repaired as well. "Now, this gonna be the room you sleep in; remember, you're just living here as a privilege. This room belongs to your daddy and me, so don't come in here!" My mother roughly explained to me. I went into the room and literally cried my eyes out while holding my bowel movement. I had no intentions of using the bathroom in a bucket, but I had no choice later that night because man, I had to poo! The smell was awful as I grabbed two buckets full of crap carrying them to the back of the house like a slave.

Can you imagine carrying urine and poo in a bucket outside the house while the inside still held the smell all in your clothing? Not to mention, I still washed all my clothes by hand in the bathtub and I had to bring the buckets back inside! Till this day, I will never take advantage of a toilet and as a matter of fact, I treat it like royalty! Well, if that's not enough, there were roaches everywhere once again but they were accompanied by every other insect the country had to offer. So we had to watch out for spiders, mosquitoes, and other insects.

Now moving forward, was my fresh start in a new school I had been enrolled in. It seemed as if things were just not going to get better for me and here I was getting ready to start a new school year as a traumatized kid in a shack of a home where I can't even claim my room. The teachers and the children I met would have no idea what I was going through and why the tears fall regularly. Amite Westside was the name of the school I attended. Every single day, as I walked into the classroom, I stayed to myself because I knew mostly everyone was talking about me negatively.

Meanwhile, at home, it took a while but the owner finally bought us a toilet and my mother fixed up the house a little better. It didn't affect me much besides the smell but I still was full of cigarette smoke going to school. One morning, as I pulled out my clothes from the dresser, I saw holes in most of them. It didn't dawn on me that moment, so I just quit thinking about it at the time. Well, when I got back home from a horrible day in school, I started reading a book when suddenly I heard something loud in the kitchen making sounds every few minutes. I was home alone like always so; I knew it wasn't my parents.

As I tiptoed to the kitchen, I peeped slowly into the door as the sound keeps coming. In amazement, I almost passed out when I saw what was sitting on the sink without a care in the world. It was two huge rats, chewing on a loaf of bread and ramen noodles they had dragged from the top of the refrigerator. O Yaa and believe me, it is possible! Guys, when I say things just couldn't get worse and to top it off, as I stood in the doorway, they kept eating!! The rats had no intentions of being scared of me. Then it dawned on me. I immediately remembered my clothes being full of holes in the dressers. It was because the baby rats were eating my clothes like food and leaving crap pellets everywhere as well! What a time to be alive folks!

Seeing that it was out of my control, and I couldn't do anything, I just went back to my room and continued reading my book. As long as we lived in that house, I always saw those rats and didn't say anything about them. I admit I was scared to eat though. The reason being that I wasn't always offered hot food my parents cooked, seeing that they believed kids don't have to eat everything the grown-ups ate. They had one hot plate as well because the house didn't have a stove either. So, I would mostly eat cold bologna sandwiches and ramen noodles, especially when my father was gone, it was the worst.

Which this would cause me to have to pick the good bread apart from the bread the rats remained. So, for ramen noodles, I did the same thing. Hey, I'm just keeping it honest with the readers, it was messed up! A ghetto life that could have killed us all. Rats are known to carry diseases supposedly too, so I can tell you I'm blessed to be telling this story! The reason for me telling the readers these things amongst going to this new school all at once is because it could become one of the worst feelings ever for a child going through all of this after the trauma-filled city life.

Amite Westside was one of the toughest experiences in my school life that I had. You see, New Orleans was where I became traumatized whereas, in Amite, I became emotional, sick, put in a worse place, and stuck. When I say stuck, I mean on pins and needles because my father and I were on a close watch by "the system» I felt. One more mess up and it probably would have cost us both. So, when I was at school, if I got picked on, I would drop my head ignoring them, cry MANY TIMES from the life I was dealing with at home, think about the trouble I'll be in if I flip out, and just try to stay humble to myself. So, as I got into more of the school side of things, I can say that it wasn't all that bad. If you think about it, no one at school knew my situation, my past, and of course, their little lives wasn't the same as mine, so they didn't know any better. Some of the boys were ballplayers since they were babies loved by their mother, the girls were spoiled, and they were both family-oriented whether they were hood or not. Joshua didn't have a single lick of that life and I couldn't tell you the first thing about a little league at the time!

What you have already read up to this point, speaks for itself throughout this book. I was so naive about the things children were participating in around me. So, the students there didn't know any better; it's just that I had my disgusting issues that they didn't have to go through. For instance, I used my "studying people tactic,» to hold close to me through these stages in my life, to help me focus on becoming smarter! I studied the kings and queens of Westside, which were the Foster family. I've never seen anything like it in my little life up until now. Nobody played around with the Fosters because it was like a hundred of them.

If you hung out with them on the regular, I considered you a Foster as well. Tina Foster was one of the finest girls I had seen at any school I'd attended and she knew it. I knew what fine was at this age thanks to hanging out with my father and she had a big butt with a beautiful smile! She was like the queen that no one messed with, and she knew everyone's business. I studied her more than anyone, and sometimes, it was as if she knew I was going through a lot. Instead of picking on me, she complimented me a lot which confused me, but I told myself I would never forget that.

Then there was her brother Bud. He was cool like her, but you can tell he had hung around girls a lot because he was messy just like them. Then there was Alan. He was like the foster family's bodyguard. In other words, nobody played with him and if they did, they probably wanted to be knocked out. Right now, I think he's still knocking people out. I never had any personal problems with Alan though. You also had the beautiful Jasmine Foster and of course, there were more but those are some of the main ones. There was also a family of Cyprian's, Bennett Road boys, Butler Town, and Hines Quarter families that were close-knit as well. I would also study the teachers and how they catered to the different families also. Well, being that I was from New Orleans and my story, I didn't fit in at all. A lot of the families knew my mother, especially in the Butler Town area. If you remember, in the beginning, my grandma used my mother in clubs as bait for older men to fish at. Well, half of those men were from some of these families, so in the past, my mother slept with many of them sometimes 5 or 6 at a time.

Today we call it running a train on a girl and my father was said to be warned about it, but he was in the streets himself, so he probably didn't pay attention to that. I also knew that in New Orleans, my father wasn't the only one cheating either. She used to tell me all the time, «Sometimes we as women have to do what we have to do so mind your damn business!» Anyways, my mother's past caused me to be the butt joke of it all at school and my parents didn't have to care about it either. There was an incident that happened a day after I was picked on about my mother that probably changed my life as far as my thinking toward friends and family.

You remember I said that I would tell you about my cousins like Elliot? Well, I'm standing alone outside while everyone else played or stood around the playground. As I was doing so, two people were looking at me giggling and pointing. It was Aaron and Anthony. Aaron and his family were known to be street people from one of the areas I told you about. The crazy part about it was one of my cousins on my mother's side, Cody, was his close friend and maybe cousin as well. Anthony was a part of the Bennet Road crew and was really close with my cousin Elliot.

Well, while they giggled and pointed directly at me, I walk up to them alone and ask them, "What you looking at me laughing for?" They didn't answer, but I knew they felt me, as they now walked away with frowns on their faces. As I stood there, all I could feel was pain and exhaustion from my troubles at home and my school messing with me. My temper had become short-fused and I had begun the process of lashing out. Although I wasn't a fighter, I knew I had slapped a few people in my time, hung with gangsters like GG, but I was relieved they walked away because my standing there gave me time to realize that I was in a different situation than them.

If they get into trouble, they will go home to their families. If I get into trouble, I may not have a home. Well, that was just my luck because Anthony had felt disrespected I guess because he doubled back with Aaron right behind him. Before I knew it, I was beaten up and I have no reason in my book to sugar coat it. What they did to me that day, didn't hurt my life any worse but all my cousins, such as Elliot and whomever else, sat back and watched. My embarrassment didn't come from being beaten up; it came from my so called family looking down on me as it happened.

The consequences made me feel even worse. We all wound up getting a form of school detention called Cop Shop, where a police officer has his own classroom, making you write hundreds of sentences and run around the school like a boot camp. So you mean to tell me, I was whipped and now I'm being punished for it? As every hour passed, I looked at the door, scared to death, thinking the people from the system was coming to get me. To my amazement, they never showed up. That was another terrible day in my life but I learned my lesson. I captured moments like this just as well as I would study them since that would take me down a cold path in my future life.

Now, remember I said that Cody was close to Aaron, right? Well, the following weekend my mother decided to go to a party at Cody's mother's house, where Elliot and Aaron would be along with some other kinfolk. My mother wasn't known to hang with other people, but since we moved back to the country, I guess she wanted to get back in touch with her family. Well, as soon as Aaron got the chance, he was the first one pointing at me with my young family behind him, laughing their ass off. The worst part is, I don't think he even had an idea he was surrounded by my family but it didn't even matter.

The whole night I just watched everyone having fun while I was sitting alone at the table confused. I was questioning why these people treated me just as bad as my mother. While I sat there, I did get a good view of Cody's mother dancing like a stripper along with some more girls. They were twerking to the song, 'Monkey on the stick.'

While on the subject though, in the future I actually started going to weddings and more parties at their house, hanging around Cody a little more. There were pictures of us in their home, but I don't know what happened with that honestly. Cody is one cousin I can't fault at all because he didn't know me at all as the others did and I honestly pray he is doing well for himself right now. I also got a chance to meet some good family members that were nice to me, such as Aunt Moosy, Uncle Zoe, Aunt Janice (whom I already kind of knew), Tangi, and a few more.

Now I know I kind of got off subject but that's the beauty of writing so let's get back to the school. Now as for Anthony, I wound up seeing him again on the Bennett Road with no hard feelings, especially when he found out that one of my good cousins named Puddin was mutual between the two of us. Besides, I took my loss with them knowing who Joshua was and what I knew for a fact they weren't. As for Aaron, I never saw him in school again and I always said there would come a time when I will see him again in the future. School would never be the same for me.

My grades went back down to the New Orleans low, and my behavior was solitary. I didn't trust anyone and these were the times I missed Big Unc, GG, and Martin you know. I had put it in my mind that I didn't have any family here and I no longer cared either. While I was having issues in school, my mother and father were still having issues at home. My father walked around the house with a blunt hanging out of his mouth while arguing with my mother. One night it was so bad that he wrapped his hand around my mother's neck in the hallway, shoving her into the wall shouting out words I can't remember.

I cried all night long and as a result, my mother shouted, "Your daddy wanna treat me like this and leave, well tell him to take you too!" She quickly threw me on the porch and slammed the door behind me! I remember like yesterday me standing on the porch as it rained all on me that night. To take cover, I slowly walked to the side of the house where this big tree was, and I laid under it all night long.

Honestly, I had been through so much at this point; I don't think I even cared. I also found out that my grandmother did the same thing to children in the family back in the day, including my mother! I got put out by my mother out in the rain, for my father's actions, but I still loved my daddy. As I woke up the next morning, I was still lying there on the ground soaked by the rain! Now, I know that you all are thinking that I should've run, I could've been bitten by something or maybe even worst. I was a strong kid at this point, and to me I always have been. You would think that my mother would come get me, but she was tired of my father and me.

Why she was tired of me was a mystery, but this was sad guys. Now, she might not have checked up on me, but four little guys ran over to me as if I were dead and asked, "Cuz you good? What are you doing out here nigga? Aunt Linda and Uncle Rene been fighting again just like our mama and daddy huh?" I was confused, I was shocked they knew my parents, but most of all they checked on me like big Unc used to. "That's Dede, Bo, Mun, and I'm Tray and you're our big cousin," he said. In amazement, I reflected on some of the weddings I went to with my mother for her side of the family. Those kids were in all of the weddings, Aunt Janice is their grandmother, and one of the girls that were dancing by Cody's house was their mother.

Also, their trailer home was right next to our shack home, and I never even knew! These were really my cousins! "So get up cuz, you're our big brother now, follow us!" Tray said as he walked away. I had never heard anyone tell me that before in my life! For them to look at me as a big brother was weird to me and although it happened so quick, I was down with it! As I got up off the ground, I look towards the house to see if my mother was looking. She still was inside probably trying to sleep, overcoming the argument from last night. I know I slept outside, but I kind of felt relieved that I wasn't inside.

So, I followed my cousins across the street into a field of full-grown strawberries! As soon as I laid eyes on them, I began to have this feeling that we weren't supposed to be there and that this was someone's property. Before I could ask, Dede blurts out, "This our kinfolk's berries cuz, so don't worry we just go pick a few. We gotta be quick though before somebody else tries to come take some with us!"

I looked at them in amazement as they picked the berries so fast and ate them at the same time as they went down the row. "Man come on and eat some cuz; I know you hungry!" Bo said with his mouth full of berries. I slowly started eating them one by one. As we got halfway down the row, a loud truck pulled up the rock road quickly towards us. "Runnnnnnnnnnnn, it's Doc! Come on man! RUNNNNN", Tray shouted as we ran like we stole something! One thing I learned in the city was that if you see other people running, you run too!

Later on, I discovered that we really were stealing. I got the true run down from my cousins that we were picking out of Doc's field of strawberries. He was a relative of their dad Darrell and the owner of the shack house I lived in. We didn't get caught that day, and my stomach was full as a tick. After I'd learned who he was, I didn't care if we ate all of his berries. He gave us a broken down house and never fixed things when it needed to be done. Not to mention, a house full of rats the size of my forearm! I remember that day in my life not only getting a chance to have actual boy cousins but getting a rundown on a lot I didn't know.

Now Mun didn't talk much, Bo and Dede were really young badasses, but Tray was the oldest out of the four. He initiated mostly everything they did, whether it be bad or good; they followed. He was years younger than me, but he was smart. Now that day, we must've sat under the tree for hours talking about anything Tray thought I needed to know. I started to dry quickly from the rain due to the sun. Aunt Janice was their grandma and she was my auntie. Their mother's name was Keisha, Janice's daughter, who was married to their father Darrel.

Those were my cousins, but since they were so much older, I called them my aunt and uncle. Now, aunt Janice was married to Uncle Terry, and they were my great aunt and uncle. He explained to me that my Grandfather was murdered in Fluker, Louisiana which was my mother's father and Janice's brother. A little different from New Orleans but I found out that the whole of my grandpa's family was ghetto and hood. Cody, Tangi, Aunt Moosey, and more were either descendants or siblings of my grandfather. My mother never gave me a rundown of my family tree so, I was confused.

I've seen these people at weddings, I've been by their houses, but I was to myself – never knowing any of them. None of these names came to the city or were invited to our house. I learned that my mother used to babysit Keisha when she was younger, also accompanied by her younger brother. I guess that's why my mother and Aunt Janice had a relationship with one another.

I never saw this happen with any other family member. As I continued to listen to Tray, he talked about how Terry would beat aunt Janice up and how my Uncle Darrel would do the same to Keisha in front of him and his brothers. Also, nights of starving with nothing to eat for them and how he had to sleep on top of a urine-filled mattress because his brothers still peed in the bed! As he expressed himself, all I could think of was my situation. I never would've thought an actual family member was going through half of what I was going through. We even talked about how most of our family was either on drugs or selling them.

"I've been stealing my daddy cigarettes from time to time, smoking them behind the trailer, sipping maw gin, and her OE bottle. I bet if you take one of aunt Linda's cigs, she gonna kill you!" Tray said laughing loudly. I told him how I would never smoke a day in my life because the smell bothered me anyways, but I could drink a 40 ounce all day long while sipping some gin right with it...That's exactly what we did too! It was amazing how these little kids, especially Tray, knew all about our family and enough about me. It was as if he waited for this day to finally talk to me.

He was the type of kid that would keep an open ear out for what grown folks were talking about. So, all he had heard, he just related it to me on this same day. He explained to me how he knew no one ever came to our house to spend the night or visit, how we were so private, them talking about the way I was treated, my father having a good soul but just in the streets, and my mother being a mean witch like my grandma. All I could think of in my mind was, "Wow! I'm from New Orleans but here, it is miles away in the country, and my mother's family seemed to know so much about us!"

You know, this is the chapter where I now start to break being so naive to things and have a more open mind. Well, now I felt I had a family to lean on once again, but this time everything will be played cool. I would often reflect on what the judge told me or what one of my teachers said about me back at home to keep me on a positive path. As time went by, I still dealt with issues at home, at school, and personally with myself. My parents would raise me to believe that all we had was each other, but I felt like all I had was my cousins next door.

My parents stayed gone together without me, making it feel like New Orleans all over again. So, I spent the majority of my time with the cuzzos, while my parents were gone. Uncle Darrel was always working, Keisha was always working as well, and Aunt Janice would come and go leaving us alone. If Aunt Janice did stay, she would always become drunk falling all around, while we laughed at her, drinking as well! We would always eat can foods without even cooking them because sometimes that's all we had to eat.

We were just some ghetto children in the country, and I was a terrible babysitter! Often, my Aunt Janice reminded me of my Grandma Helen the way she talked about my mother as my mother would do the same. I would sit back and ask myself, "How can they all talk about each other but never confront each other in person?" My mother would even let her borrow money that was never paid back, they would sit for hours and talk about things, but when they split up, it's as if they hated each other! It was starting to come to me that my mother's side of the family was just mean and hateful but wanted to do better with good intentions if that makes any sense.

My mother was also super strict with her own family. For instance, one day, my father was gone and my mother had to leave for just a few hours. Before she left, she held my arm aggressively saying, "Now, don't you let anybody into this house you hear me! I don't want to have to come back and my stuff gone, so go to your room until I come back! I don't care if they're lost and have to use the bathroom, don't let them in!" I heard her loud and clear as I slowly walked to my room and sat on the floor. At the time my cousins were gone, so once again I was alone for the day. About an hour passed and I heard a knock at the door. "Josh? This is Keisha boy open the door; I got to make a serious phone call! I know you in there so come on! I gotta use the phone boy," she shouted.

I felt like it was so wrong to leave her out there knowing all she needed was the phone, so I opened the door! "Damn boy, what took you so long?" She asked. "My mama says I'm not supposed to let anybody into the house or ima get in trouble for real!" I replied while looking out the front door praying she would hurry up! It wasn't like she knew what kind of trouble I would be in any way, so it didn't matter. She finally made her phone call for a ride somewhere. This was back in the 90s still, so cell phones weren't that popular.

She glanced at my facial expression back and forth as she looked through my mother's movie tapes. "I know if I take one of these tapes, Linda gonna kill both of us and you look scared as hell boy, let me go! That's a damn shame how they treat you because you've been through more than you'll ever know," she said seriously, as she walked back to her house. All I felt was a sigh of relief as I put my back against the wall, slid down slowly and sat on the floor. As I sat there, all I could think about was Keisha saying, "More than you'll ever know!"

I couldn't think long because suddenly, my mother pulled up and ran inside. By the time she got inside, I was already back into my room, sitting on the floor and not saying a word about what I'd done. "Come on here boy and sit on the porch. I need to cut your head because it looks bad," she said. That's right folks. At that time, as a kid, I didn't know what a barber was! The same goes for my father as well because my mother cut our hair. An embarrassing bowl of a haircut sitting on my head and a square-shaped jerry curl on my father's head! So, as we were sitting outside, I thought the rest of the day might go well.

As I was getting my head jacked up, a car slowly pulled up at my cousin's house blowing the horn numerously. Keisha walked out of the house, jumps in it and they pulled off. As I was sitting there, my heart felt like it had fallen to my feet, and I froze like a stop sign. My mother asked curiously, "How she get a damn ride somewhere she ain't got no phone?" I sat there speechless, continuing to freeze as she talked to herself. Finally, she gave me the same look she would give me when she felt like I was telling a lie for my father. "Did you let her in my house? I told you nobody; I don't care if they're family or not I meant that s#$%!

Now did you or did you not let her in here?" She asked already knowing the answer. My response was a nod "No" to her, but she still wasn't buying it. She quickly finished jacking my head up and pulled me inside whipping me nonstop as if I had committed a crime saying, "You lie just like your daddy boy! You wanna let people into my house when you barely stay here! What the hell is wrong with you?" As I said before, the whippings had become numb to me, but the words she said had become like knives cutting deeply. Before I knew it, my father had come home, she talked to him, and I got beaten again.

He had reopened the wounds that my body had from the first whipping! Later that night when it was all over, I was in my room when my father came in and apologized to me. I cried heavily as he walked out. I was confused about why I had been beaten so badly, what Keisha meant about what she said, and my life period. Life would seem good at moments while hanging with my cousins, but moments like these make my mind revert to everything bad that has happened to me. Attending school and being at home were not my favorite things to do at all. Little did I know, my life was getting ready to change into another chapter.

A chapter is far more different than the others but so revealing to many of my questions. Well, months later, as I walk slowly down the rock road, all I could think about were the punishment I was going to receive due to my low grades. As the bus drove away behind me, I made it the slowest walk home ever! When I made it home, my parents were gone, and my cousins were outside waiting on me. "Ay cuz I heard y'all finna move! Aunt Linda told maw maw Janice y'all gone in a few months." Tray said as he shook his head. I replied confused saying, "You know I don't know cuz, they never tell me nothing anyways. I wish I could just stay with y'all!"

Tray started to smile sneakily, "Don't I know cuz! I wish you could too. You're our big homie, and you don't know nothing. Come inside my momma nem wanna see you." I walk into the house accompanied by the rest of my cousins, Keisha, and my Aunt Janice looking at me as if something just happened. "Don't forget about us when you move now. Y'all finna move out there across the river in the country by them white folks! You ain't gone be used to that no boy!" Aunt Janice said with a grin on her face.

As soon as she said that my heart stopped and all I could think about was moving once again. Although I didn't like it at first, I finally found family again with my cousins here on James Rd. «Why we have to move now?» I thought. I had forgotten all about my terrible report card, especially after Keisha and Aunt Janice told me something that changed my life. "Look at the marks on your arms and legs! I'm so sorry I came over there to use that phone.

Josh, have you ever asked yourself why your mama treats you the way she does? Do certain things in your life make you just wonder why? Just Why?" Asked Keisha softly. To every question she asked, I stood there saying yes to everyone one of them. I could feel the energy in the room going down, the television I tuned out, and any other sound was muted.

I had no idea this day would be another moment towards changing my life, but I knew something big was about to be said! As Aunt Janice lit up her cigarette and took a sip of her gin, she softly swallowed and said to me loudly, "Them ain't your real damn parents!

Your real mama was too young to take care of you and Rene ain't your damn daddy! They should have told you before you got this age so you won't be looking like you're looking right now! We shouldn't have told you either but hell I couldn't hold it anymore boy them folks doing you bad over there. You walking around here all lost. I'm surprised you ain't gone crazy yet! You were adopted as a young boy in New Orleans. I'm sorry baby, bless your heart!" My cousins that showed me the most attention I'd ever had were now looking at me with long faces quiet as ever as I stood speechless.

Although I had no idea what it meant entirely, the only thing I could hear repeatedly was, "You were adopted and them ain't your real parents!" At that moment, the story of my life just entered a new chapter!

CHAPTER 8

THE ADOPTION

"Adopting one child won't change the world, but for that one child the world will change!"
- Author Unknown

With about eight weeks left in the school year, I was just a kid in class that didn't care about nothing at all. I was lost, confused, and just like everything else, I kept this to myself as well. I never told anyone what I was going through. My grades were rock bottom, I was still the butt joke in school, and to top it off, I got kicked out of my homeroom class until further notice. There was a substitute teacher by the name of Ms. Edwards that filled in for the day. Well, let's just say I was sitting right next to a couple of people that were cutting up in the classroom.

To make a long story short, I took the blame for their actions, Ms. Edwards believed it, and I was sent to the office along with Tory, one of Aaron's friends. Tory received a paddling from the principle whereas, I received suspension until they speak with one of my parents. Instantly, I thought back to how back at home, they did a similar thing to me in order to reach my parents. The school wanted my parents' attention about my grades, lack of participation, and my solitary actions. They knew I wasn't a bad kid, but they obviously sensed that something was wrong.

This happened after finding out the biggest thing in my life just a few weeks ago. Of course, my mother never went to the school house, so my father went after I told him what happened. He went to the school and got his head full of my doings and how the teachers were concerned for me.

Well, when it was all over, I found out that what my cousins had told me about me moving was true. After my father's conference with the school, I would never step foot on West Side middle school campus again. In fact, I never even had a chance to tell my lil cousins/my brothers bye, the lovely queen Tina, the sexy Robin Warford I had a secret crush on, and the beautiful Dashema Toefield who had the best smile.

Those were just some of the people I paid close attention to that I didn't get to say goodbye. I was taken straight to our new home in the middle of the woods. A trailer home surrounded by country land, horses, and more trailers. The whole ride there, my father didn't say not one word to me, so I knew what time it was. He told me to wait inside in the back room and take all my clothes off. Thirty minutes later, I had received the worst beating ever with a long brown extension cord. It was so bad that he was hitting blisters he had already made, and bumps started forming on my arms and legs because of it.

Imagine that kind of whipping right after learning you were adopted, but you didn't know what it fully meant so you just kept quiet about it. Secondly, I got in trouble for something I didn't do, but I didn't say anything. That was another charge to the game and I kept it solid. I just curled up in the new room they gave me and closed my eyes tight wishing I could leave the world. Wishing I could not live anymore. I was scared to run away because of my earlier experience with Martin.

At that moment GG and Unc crossed my mind; that bullet crossing my shoulder, dead bodies I've seen, the hurtful words my mother would tell me, the blunts hanging out my father's mouth, the different crack houses

I sat in front of, the different women I encountered, my family that hated to be around me, roaches and rats, being picked on by those who have a family, the unanswered questions I have no answer to, and I can keep going forever.

I remember as I balled up in pain, I asked myself, "WHY ME!?" Later that night, my mother came to the back room to look at me and I could hear her asking my father, "Why the hell you whip him so badly?" I couldn't hear his response as they walked back to the other side of the trailer. Later that night, as I got off the floor, I felt a sudden burst of energy, so I sneakily walked outside still swollen. I had heard the Quinns, I mentioned earlier in the story, talk about God and we also went to a Jehovah's Witness Kingdom Hall a few times. So, I was familiar with asking him for things if I had no one else to turn to.

Secondly, I remembered being locked in my room reading my book of Bible stories trying to teach myself things in my own way. So, I walk to the backfield where it was pitch dark and I closed my eyes, and I talked to God saying, "God or whoever you are. I believe you are real and I have read plenty of books about you as well to believe you are. I pray that my situation changes and that you keep me from giving up and that I don't stray the wrong way.

I've been through some tuff stuff that no one around me seems to have been through. Last but not least, why was I adopted, and what does it fully mean God? Please answer my questions before I go crazy! PLEASE!" I looked around slowly, and I ran back to the trailer and back into the back room.

At this point, I was just about tired of using the pliers to switch the television or beating it on the side of it to put it on. Besides, I was still swollen from that beating earlier, so I decided to lay down and try to sleep. As I woke up the next morning, there was complete silence throughout the trailer. I peeked out of the bedroom door and the window, to see that my parents were gone as usual. All I could think of was my damn auntie replaying in my head and the beating I received yesterday for being falsely accused. Well, like everything else, I shrugged it off and took a walk outside whether they allowed me or not!

Now, of course, I had been outside already, but this particular day I just stared at everything in sight. The different fruit trees, the long dirt road, a barb wire fence, horses walking, cows eating, the old man picking vegetables off of his land, a big white boat broke down in the backfield, the peaceful sounds of birds chirping, and a long line of rusty green filled old trailers.

Man, it looked like a peaceful ghetto country – better known as trailer park trash! I finally started to walk towards the back of our trailer where there was a barb wire fence blocking a huge field with one ugly little trailer and two big horses.

As I walked closer to the fence to be nosey, I smelled something all too familiar that lit my nose up! "Daddy must be around somewhere cuz I smelled the weed!" I thought. I was wrong. As I was looking around, three white boys were headed my way as I quickly tried to run and go back inside. "Hey wait up, we're not gonna bite you!" Said one of them. "What's your name lil bruh?" He asked as he inhaled a white paper full of weed. "Um, I'm ah... Josh!" I replied back, stuttering. "Well you can call me Mr. Bum, this is my son Raymond, and this is my baby boy Ryan. Can we call you JJ?" Mr. Bum asked as he was still enjoying his blunt. "Yaa that's kool. Well, I gotta get back inside before my people nem get back home hea!" I said to them as I steadily looked back for my pops. "Ok! You a city boy I hear it all in your voice.

Well, you go head on inside. My boy Raymond here is about your age so why don't y'all hang out soon JJ and hey nice to meet you." As he walked away backward talking to me high as a kite. I proceeded to nod my head and back in the house I went to. I wasn't used to talking to white people where I was from unless it was the system. Besides, my mother talked bad about them, so I believed whatever she said. Here I was, sitting in my room once again looking at the four corners of the walls all day and all night long.

My parents were working at their new job together, Sanderson Farm. Since they also shucked oysters, they were familiar with that type of work. Anyways, I wasn't allowed to go in the fridge for food, the kitchen, nor the living room for television, ever. As my stomach growled, all I could think of was my mother's mean ass, my father who could no longer sneak me food, and what my school would be like when I started. Finally, my thoughts were interrupted by a loud opening of the front door. It was them coming through the door. In the trailer, it was carpet on the floor so, you could hear when someone was walking to the room I stayed in.

My mother appeared at the door saying, "You getting your ass back in school tomorrow so get your stuff ready so you can go to bed. Your daddy bought you some nice shoes from Payless since there ain't no KMart down here. Shouldn't have bought your ass nothing and let you keep wearing them tore up shoes you done messed up. Hurry up so you can go to bed!" "Can I get something to eat?" I asked under my breath. My mother gave me a death stare and replied, "You don't deserve nothing, acting up in that damn classroom!" Before I could flinch, I was slapped in my face three times by her reminding me of the beating I had received the day before.

Now, I write about this particular time in my book because something had come over me at an instant as I stood there holding my face. I mean I get falsely accused, I got beaten like always, I'm clueless on adoption and them not being my parents, I'm tired of wearing shoes that last maybe two weeks, being the butt joke at every school, and getting slapped for no reason. I was fed up with taking up for my daddy after all I've done for him, and to top it all; I was tired of STARVING! The tears rolled down my face, but this time slowly and barely.

I may have been too young to understand rage at that age, but I did understand that something else was inside of me. As if I had another person in me or an altered ego. The sorrow and cry baby mentality I felt for myself, would begin to turn into strong anger at a very young age. It would start to unfold as my story goes on but for now, I played it all cool.

I'm talking about playing it cool like I used to do for my father holding him down years in a row with his infidelities. Reading all those books and dealing with an exposed life growing up, gave me a different kind of instinct. It was an advantage that helped me to make a decision on this day, to somehow bury my past. New Orleans would eventually become half erased from my mind but never forgotten, the adoption thoughts would slowly fade as well, and my sad, quiet attitude would eventually change. I couldn't sleep that night.

Something was telling me that would be the last time I would get slapped, whipped, and touched at all by my parents or anybody else for that matter. Joshua was done! I decided to go into this new school humbly. I will say that the books I read gave me power in my mind as a kid. My Auntie was exactly right. They couldn't have been my parents treating me like this and secondly, I was a young strategic thinker that didn't know much, but I knew enough to know that I would get through this. "You're smarter than you think Joshua. You can be someone and one day you will get anything you want.

You'll be able to eat anything you desire. Please don't give up. I know it is tough but just be patient son!" A voice said in my head that same night as I was lying down facing the wall. I'm serious guys, this is true and it still freaks me out! Crazy weird feelings with some amazing thoughts that night, which would stick with me for the rest of my life. I was becoming someone or something I couldn't understand just yet, but time will tell, trust me!

The next morning as you all know by now, I was a pro with getting up for school. The routine didn't change much of course and I was off to the bus stop right up the dirt road. Weirdly to me, Raymond and his brother Ryan were at the bus stop. Man I was confused because I had never seen white people riding the bus before!

"What's up man, how you doing?" Asked Raymond as his brother looked at me, smiling from ear to ear. "You don't talk much do you?" He asked. I just shook my head from side to side in reply like always. "Well, that's ok. My dad talked to your dad and it looks like y'all are gonna be here in the trailer park for a while so we can be friends aight!" Raymond replied as I said «Okay» directly back to him. He continued to ask me if I liked to play football, and I looked at him confused.

Yes people, I had no idea about football at the time growing up. All I knew about was Christy the ice skater and basketball because my dad played a lot. Well, as the bus pulled up, Raymond looked at me saying, «I will teach you every day after school in our big yard, I promise you.» All I could think about was the friends I had lost, my little cousins/brothers, and so-called family members that treated me like an outsider. Last night though, my thoughts told me, I had to bury the pain and move on. So, I accepted it.

I was the last one to walk slowly onto the bus as not only the new kid but the last kid the bus would pick up on its route. So, you know that meant a full bus. Guys, to my surprise, it was filled with nothing but black people! «Unbelievable here in this trailer park country,» I thought as I was being stared down by everyone, as I walked slowly trying to find a seat. I finally got to take a seat by this beautiful heavy set dark skinned girl. I forget her name but she was way older than me. At the time she was already in high school.

You see, Raymond and a few others would ride this bus to a different school than I was attending due to their grade levels. Raymond and his brother were the only white people on the bus to my surprise. A few other kids and I would get dropped off first at Chesbrough Elementary whereas, they would continue to Jewel Sumner High School, further down from my new school. Chesbrough was a very small rural school and so was Sumner. There wasn't a store or hospital to be found for miles away so if you needed something or you got hurt, good luck!

Little did I know at this point in my life, that these country areas were also tough environments like back at home. Well, as I got off the school bus, I stood still in amazement at how freaking small the school was man. This was the size of daycare in New Orleans. That reminds me even more that I wasn't just some ordinary kid. You see, the stuff I paid attention to, other kids around me didn't. I was so used to being poor and never being equal to others, that it caused me to look at things in life differently than the next kid.

I noticed the kids were even dressed differently than in the city. I basically paid attention to everything moving and standing still! Ryan got off the bus still smiling. He had a bad ADHD problem, so he had to take Ritalin all the time! His mother stayed in the schoolhouse on a weekly basis for his behavior and from beating people up. I don't want to get ahead of myself before I tell you the rest of my first day.

"Ok. I'm going to do better with my behavior and my grades. I will keep my life secret and my adoption silent. I will not ask questions about adoption. I will not worry about my parents and again, no adoption Josh!" I kept saying to myself over and over again as I finally walked into the school. I was shown to the office where I was immediately taken to my class. On the way, a teacher asked if I had eaten anything. I just froze as if I had seen a ghost because I've never been asked that before at home from my mother! I was in shock she even cared. I finally snapped out of it and shook my head «no» quickly.

She took me to breakfast where I ate like I was starving! Shortly after I was done, I entered my new classroom with a mixed crowd of black and white kids. Like I said before, I wasn't used to seeing that! The teacher introduced me and afterward, I sat in the back of the class. Everyone was pretty tense because Leap testing was going on that entire week. Leap is a test taken in Louisiana by all students in order to test the knowledge we had on all subjects in the 6th grade and in the 11th grade if I'm not mistaken.

It determined whether we would go to the next grade or not. I had no idea about it, and I was not ready, but I remembered what I had told myself. On our break, we were allowed to go outside for a while to catch a breather. That was when life took yet another turn for me. "Say bruh I heard you were from New Orleans! How many brothers you got? Why your arms all scratched up? He's been trying to tattoo himself. Yea probably so, you know them New Orleans cats crazy!" Different people said as they crowded around me. I stood there shy as hell but smiling at all the questions and accusations.

I also knew that the scratches on my arm were from that beat down I took from my father but never again. One by one they started introducing themselves to me. Paris, Kenny Jackson, Bj Dyson, Jeremy, Craig Fox who didn't talk very much and last but not least, the head dude in charge, Charlie Fox. Now you may be asking why him. Charlie Fox was said to be nothing to play with. His family was known to be deep like the Fosters in Amite. He was also the cousin of Craig Fox, and none of them was scared of anything.

They were about that life as Charlamagne Tha God says. Also, he was great in physical performance and sports. That was a subject I knew nothing about. To top it off, he got his first tattoo in fourth grade! Yes, you heard me people! Fourth-grade man that's crazy but Charlie Fox did it. I'm probably missing someone right now but let's get on with the story anyways. There were two more girls I did remember in my class, Jessica who was foreign from Belize and Alicia Hemingway! They were some of the 'top of the class' students and later, I would join them. That's right people!

Mr. Joshua Jackson was no longer a low-grade scrub. I decided to push out my full potential, and they also taught a little different in the country, making it a bit easier for me to understand I guess. I only had six weeks of school left when I attended Chesbrough prior to the West Side situation. So I had to do my best. I passed the leap test and for that, I was able to attend Sumner with everyone else. Still, after everyone talking to me, I never spoke my past truth, and I still kept my adoption situation silent. With the improved way I was acting and the past cover up I'd done, I fit right in with my class like normal.

I didn't hear or see any murders around the trailer or at school; I didn't have to jump on the floor for any cover from bullets flying, no bounce music with twerking battles at school, and no worries of seeing my father in The Times-Picayune for wrongful doings. Now don't get it twisted, I was still the poor broke down butt joke of a kid but at least it wasn't as bad as it used to be and by now I was used to it!

The last day of school, I told all my new classmates goodbye, and little did I know, I would grow with them for years to come. Life started to change for me in shall I say a different, "opening way" that started yet another chapter becoming more interesting. Things like sports, work, girls, mindset, religion, and lessons made my story so much better as each chapter unfolds with me as I grow!

CHAPTER 9

THE LESSONS LEARNED WHILE GROWING

"The turning point in the process of growing up is when you discover the core strength within you that survives all hurt!
- Max Lerner

"Hey JJ, run out for a long one! I'm going to throw it to you deep bro!" Raymond told me as I started to run full speed down his huge field of a yard. He had thrown the football perfectly to me, and I missed it! "That's ok bro, we're going to keep working on it but you're getting much better." I ran back to him smiling and he continued to push me over and over again until I became good at it.

Raymond taught me the game of football, basketball, and how to work out at my age. We became good friends and normally, I would hook up with him when I was done working with my father on the weekends. At 6:00 am every Saturday, my father would wake me out of my sleep saying to me, "Son? Son? It's time to go to work now cuz ain't nobody gonna give us nothing free.

Now I want you to be ready by the time I load up this truck hea?" I sat there at the edge of my bed or shall I say their bed, in that room every Saturday looking up at him wishing he would just cancel for one weekend. I was doing this work ever since I was six years old, and by the time I was at Sumner High, I was tired. Celebration station never came for me after being promised so many times.

I never once set my feet in the sand next to blue water or rode on a roller coaster. I had never been anywhere outside of my sheltered zone ever! I remember vividly each time my parents would leave to take vacation trips. If they weren't on a plane trip, they were in a limo dressed to kill, or my daddy would do over and beyond for my mother in little small getaways.

Which he should do because he was still putting her through hell! You can guess where I was each time though. That's right! I would be right at home! As a result of never doing different things and never experiencing different places, my mentality stayed hood. You know what though, at this point in my life, I had become numb to the fact. Telling me hurtful things like they didn't feel like being bothered with any kids during their getaways, as if I begged to be here. I used to think maybe something was wrong with me, which was occasional since New Orleans but as I said, I started to get over these big things in my life a lot quicker now.

One thing I will say is that working with my father wouldn't be in vain. I mean, I have to be honest, I learned a few lessons that actually carried me through my life. Lesson one was never to be lazy and always work hard no matter what you do. Turn your inner beast on and work harder than the rest! When he would ask me to take a break I would keep going, if I got stung by bees or rained on, I'd keep going, if I got tired I turned it up a notch.

Since I was just a kid at the time, one of the reasons why I worked so hard and fast was because I got the privilege to play ball with Raymond, every time we got finished early.

Secondly, I HATED working so I would try to get finished as fast as I could! I was looking forward to playing ball every weekend, seeing that I was so locked up all the time. Now that I think about it at this age, the best comparison I could give you is I was like an inmate that got 2 hours out of the cell to work and play ball then back in I go. It's funny to me now but I know there's a reader out there that feels the pain I felt at the time.

Lesson two would be, having your own business is the bomb.com! Nothing else is like coming, leaving, breaking, and working on your own time telling yourself what to do while making income. A few quick stories for you if I can remember.

My father and I were cutting a lady's yard next door to my grandmother Helens house at the time when all of a sudden, my father looked at me and shouted, "Come here son, you look tired let me give you some of this medicine!" He quickly goes into his cooler, pulls out two small pony beers and asked me to turn them in the air! Guys when you are on your own time you can do whatever you want but I just wouldn't recommend drinking while driving a ride lawn mower in the heat.

When I jumped back on the mower after drinking those to beers, I was high as a kite swirling through the yard finishing it slowly, while my daddy laughed at the top of his lungs at me. I loved him but he was just a bad influence man! He kept alcohol in his cooler while working and we had some good times in the heat but it never stopped us from working hard. So the next story messes me up till this day.

At the time, I was just a kid, so I did not start to understand this until I had gotten older. I was in the back room like always, but my door was cracked slightly. My father walked in after a hard day's work at his regular job at the time, looked at my mother and said, "Hey my honey, how was your day, my sweet piece of candy?" "It was ok I'm just tired as hell that's all. How was yours, walking in here all happy and smiling?" She asked, looking at him with a puzzled face. "Well, it was ok! I tell you what; it's even better now that I've quit! I let them go honey.

They tried to tell me when and how long I could take my break and I don't play with that. I politely told them thank you for your time and I left!" He answered joyfully as if he wasn't finna get beat up verbally from my mother. As I sat their giggling nonstop in my room, you can hear a penny drop on the carpet because it was so silent. Shortly afterward, my mother was on the other end, adding a curse word to every sentence!

She was trying to explain to my father that he couldn't keep quitting jobs but in her own disturbing way. My father had also quit the chicken farm a few months after that event took place as well, asking my mother as he walked off the job, "You coming honey cuz I'm out! I'm not pulling these chickens anymore I'm sorry." She refused to leave and she continued to work there. These stories, along with many more, allowed me to learn that owning your own business, will open your mind up when trying to work in the corporate world.

The knowledge of owning will have a person never wanting to work for corporate America! As I said in the beginning, my father's grandfather passed the business owning gift down to all of his children and their children. So that caused my father to be a hustler on his own time. That brings me to lesson three and that was to always remember to one day find a love to hustle! "You may have to continue to work on a job but always hustle on the side until it surpasses what you make I don't care what it is son! Yeah, school alright but you wanna get the money. I always told you, you're smart son and you can do anything you want to do, but work hard at whatever you do." These were his exact words. I told you guys, no matter how jacked up my father was, he dropped gems that last forever!

Now, as you've noticed, my story has changed a little bit for the better it seems, or it's not such a negative story anymore. I've moved to the country, I'm in a new school where people actually talk to me, my parents are getting along a little better now, there are no more killings/drugs, I'm over the adoption rumor, and my new friend is white! Well, you noticed wrong people hahaha!!! When we worked in those yards, my father was still the biggest player there was!

He was a Jackson and the family of Jackson's were ruthless when it came to other women. He just did it more silently now. I think my mother knew and she held a serious grudge that caused her to bring up old wounds endlessly. My white friend Raymond wasn't any different than Martin back in the day. He was like a black white person beating everyone up, including his little brother. I felt like I had a bodyguard if anyone tried to play with me from this point on! He also did heavy drugs with his whole family.

Secondly, people were still getting killed although it was the country and my parents were still into drugs, they think I had no idea. Nah, nobody would put anything past little Joshua because I knew. All the long trips out to Independence on Hano Rd to deal with their contact whose name I will not mention in this book. He was an older smooth type of guy. He used to walk through the woods with my father as they talked, did what they needed to do, and I would be right there with them.

They would try to speak in code in front of me, but, I was too educated at my age to miss anything they were saying. I mean come on, I grew up around it since the age of three so, give me a break hahaha! Hano Rd was one of the most drug-infested places in the parish besides a few others and I believe it still is till this day. I'll get more into that side of things and how I knew later. I want to talk a little bit about religion before I go back to the school setting because I've only touched on it a few times in this book.

It will tie the story in on my explanation of why I haven't been talking negative when I was still going through the same things. So, my parents got a knock on the door while living in the hood in New Orleans when I was very little. Now I can't remember much but to keep my book authentic as possible; I'll tell you all I know. They let these people in, and they talked for a while. I want to say that I believe both my parents were childhood Baptist, which would be the only religion they knew.

Well, as the people left the house, they gave my mother a few books and brochures to read, and they invited them to come to the Kingdom Hall. Nice people that referred to themselves as Jehovah Witnesses and the Kingdom Hall being their place of worship. Well to fast forward a little, I started seeing those same two people every week even if we moved, talking to my parents more and more. Finally, they gave in and we visited the Kingdom Hall of Jehovah Witnesses. What made it so interesting was I didn't know who God was or Jehovah seeing that I had never been to any church before.

What I will tell you is that I knew of Jehovah because all those books and brochures my parents were given, I read them. So, when I walked into that Hall, it was as if I knew the place. Unfortunately, just like he wasn't at home, my father wouldn't attend with us much to the Kingdom Hall when we went.

I remember times when I would wake my mother up, just so she could take me and also because she said she would beat me to sleep if I didn't. I was excited to go because the people were nice, I got to be out of my room, and it did something to me when the man on stage would talk and move the crowd.

I didn't care about the Jehovah part, the religion itself, and at the time the no holiday celebrating part because we were too broke to celebrate them anyways. I mainly focused on the speaker, and I would envision myself being him. I would put myself in his position with my little imagination, as the people clapped for me and made me feel good about myself.

The religion was very strict in many ways and they called it "The Truth." The two people that introduced my parents to it were Mr. and Mrs. Quinn. These two people coached and saved my parents' marriage numerous times and for that, I know they are grateful. I spoke earlier in the book about one of the biggest moments when my mother was going to kill my father.

Well, they came running over the next day right before me and my mother became homeless and skipped town. My Father dibbed and dabbled in the religion and you can tell he wanted to change, but it was tough for him. I've seen times where he'd be strung out sitting in the Hall trying to listen and pay attention and my mother likewise. It wasn't until we moved and came to the country that they would become serious about it. One day, sitting by my grandmother's house with them, they just came to the conclusion that they wanted to change their lives for the better.

One of my grandmother's next door neighbors I always paid attention to growing up. Mr. and Mrs. Winters were their names. I remember the wife because she threatened to call the police on whoever placed me in the woods for punishment after I had received a beat down for peeing outside in front of all the girls. The Winters were a couple similar to the Quinns becoming mentors to my parents. So, they decided to walk over to their home and knock on the door. From that day moving forward, life started to change for all of us. They started to re-establish themselves into the religion but this time a lot more!

I say all of us because they were a lot stricter on me and they became distant from their family members. Now, their relationship became slightly better in their marriage, but things for me had gotten worse. I watched them treat the family on both sides with a long spoon creating distance, no longer going to holiday events, no longer stepping in a church during funerals even for a family member, becoming more private than they already were, but they still smoked weed and mama still smoked her cigarettes hahaha.

I guess that's what it means to not be perfect. Also, the religion just gave them more confirmation to not celebrate my birthday and not let me partake in any holidays! The next downfall for me because of this religion, was them stressing to me even more about, «we all we got.» "Me, you, and your mama is all we got son, no one else. No one else gonna give you nothing, or do anything for you like we can do for each other." He said numerous times. I think with that being said to me over and over, by the time I had become a teenager, I didn't need anybody anymore. I had been raised to think of no family and just think of myself and Jehovah.

Secondly, I learned even more on how to keep everything a secret, as if I were a Russian spy! Still till this day, it affects me. I already didn't have a relationship with both sides of the family, but this just created more distance between us all. With me being told I was adopted and that these weren't my parents as I grew into this life, it all tied into one big knot for me. "Ok, so I've never celebrated my birthday, no more Christmas dinners by my grandmother right, they have issues even more now, we have to go to the hall 3 times a week, I wear the same suit every time, and the chains on my lockdown, just got tighter on me because of this!"

I thought to myself deeply one day as I sat in my room. They called this religion the Truth. Now notice when we were living in New Orleans, my Father was missing in action. This time around he wasn't playing any games people! My father took the religion serious, and he told me recently that he felt like Jehovah had spoken to him saying, "Put away the drugs son and learn to practice self-control!" When my father heard that voice, he immediately quit everything cold turkey and became a baptized Jehovah Witness even before my mother did.

Now, I know you are probably thinking how the hell did that happened, but it's true. The most inspiring thing about this religion is that I truly believe it was for my Father because it changed his life for the better. It put him in place in life that kept him home more, treated my mother better, and best of all, it helped build a relationship with him and me.

Would you guys believe that I Joshua Jackson, taught a grown man how to read! That's right, when my father joined the religion he came in the room shy as ever asking, "Son, do you mind teaching me how to read?" Hours we would spend together as I drilled him on how to read, how to present to the crowd and everything my mother taught me harshly about hand gestures! So, everyone that's enjoying him speaking today guys, that was me behind the scenes as a still troubled kid going with the flow! No matter what I was going through, I still taught my father how to be a fluent reader! As for my mother, she would eventually get baptized years later after letting go of those cigarettes and curse words.

Well partially, because she put a dollar in a jar every time she cursed and she still smoked weed closed off in her bedroom secretly. The years before she got baptized was a serious challenge for me but we'll get into that later on as well. Meanwhile, all this going on about religion, lessons I'm learning, the cutting off of family fully, my unanswered questions about adoption that I hid, and me becoming older was creating more of a confused distance in me.

I felt like I didn't belong with them, the religion, the stuff they were still doing silently, and I was growing older but still dealing with my pain! Now, as I was getting ready to enter high school, a series of events happened that played a big part in my future as well. I wouldn't call them lessons, but I learned a lot from them. I want the readers to know that I was doing my best to stay on track and not be all over the place in my story.

Ok, I was a little older now and my father was letting his brothers know that I was a great worker. Now, his side of the family all moved years ago to the Dallas/Fort Worth area. The only time I would regularly see them is if someone passed away in the family. That's why they are not mentioned much in my book. They would all get together and come to Louisiana for funeral arrangements. Well, this time around, I was able to go to them for working purposes. So my parents drove me to Texas to work with my Uncle Stanford and my Uncle Roy.

It was a summer vacation where I would be living with my grandmother Mildred, my Aunt Neecee, and my cousins Puddin and Pumpkin. Pumpkin was a college ball player in school, so I didn't see him much. My grandmother was sick at the time, so my aunt took great care of her. Puddin was the cousin that traveled down to Amite Bennett Rd all the time because her father's family was all from there and she was close to them. Now, as I started working with my Uncle Stanford and my Uncle Roy during the week, I was also allowed to go over to my other family members' home, Aunt Debra, Uncle Mack, Montreal, and Shemetrius.

This situation was another life-changing part of my story because I had been sheltered so long from anything you would think of, to all of a sudden in the state of Texas making money and being surrounded by family that treated life differently, which I didn't understand at all.

It felt like the time I'd just started school earlier in my story, and all the kids in the hood were getting this warm attention as I stood back in amazement. Now, it was one thing to stay with aunt Neecee and work with my Uncles, but it was another life to witness going to Uncle Mac's house. Man I never wanted to leave, and it was so fun, I had no time to tell them anything about what I was going through. If I weren't working, I would either be going to track meets with Meme, swimming competitions with Montreal, or Six Flags.

I used to think they were rich for real! The way they presented themselves and moved around was totally different from the rest of our family. It changed my life completely and my whole thought process. You guys I mean, they showed me a different style of living. I felt like I was in a movie playing in a happy family role. Sure they probably had problems, but they were nothing like mine I promise you! I had become close to all of my cousins while staying there and, everyone would start to question me on certain things they knew I was going through, even religion.

Once again, I stayed quite not saying much at all. This was the summer I got a chance to witness all of my father's family members first hand, and it was amazing. I wanted to be around a cousin like Pumpkin that took me to the mall and taught me manly stuff for the first time in my life. I wanted to be around a person like Puddin to argue with all the time playfully or around an aunt like Debra and Neecee that gave me wisdom on certain things that was not being taught to me. It was as if I had stepped into a whole different world!

I brought that mentality back with me to the country in Louisiana after that summer stay. Before I was able to do that, my mother was at it again. When I stopped working with my uncle, I was barely a teenager but I thought I got paid pretty well. Well, when my parents arrived to get me, my mother pulled me to the side asking, "Where all the money you made?» I think it would've been better if she could have told me she missed me, she loved me, or even give me a hug, but she didn't. "You heard me boy, where's the money and how much did you make?" She asked again more aggressively. I admittedly started crying as I lifted open my shoe box and she took all of the $1500 I had made over the summer and did not live me a dime of it.

That hurt my heart so bad at that moment I couldn't hold my tongue any more as I blurted out, "So you gonna smoke my money up or gamble it?" She stepped back in amazement at my lash out and responded, "I take care of you nigga you don't take care of me!" I looked back up at her with a devilish stare and I asked boldly, "why you gotta gamble up all the money I make? I thought you quit all that?" I was full of confidence that day and pissed off at the same time.

I was supposed to be beaten that day but that was the part of me that wasn't naive. You see, I'd studied her enough to know she wasn't going to do anything to me because she knew in her heart she was wrong. Instead of apologizing before she walked off, she answered me saying, "You think you smart don't you boy? Well, you don't know a damn thing, and I put this money wherever I need it to be!" I sat there in pain as she walked away not caring at all. I never saw that money again, and I later found out she was back gambling in the Amite area back in Louisiana.

I had been through my father telling me, "I don't have to pay you anything; I'm the one taking care of you boy." That would be his phrase when I worked with him but that wasn't my father talking; that was my mother controlling him. I hate to say this but he was a yes man, and she was the dominant trait in the house. My father did my mother wrong for so long that, it was an obligation to him that she stays happy, whether she was right or wrong. I suffered for years behind this and I also learned from all of these events as well.

I could never keep money. She even took me to open a bank account for young people called a piggy bank account. It never kept money in it because she spent it all. I wanted to go back and live happily ever after in Fort Worth, but unfortunately, it was the other way around. My cousin Pumpkin wound up getting killed on a motorcycle accident not too long after my summer down there, and after that, I pretty much lost touch with that side until another funeral came.

It had really begun to be just us three, especially after another event happened. This time, it would be my mother's side of the family. She had stopped talking to Cody's people, Aunt Janice and Keisha, and some more of her family. This right here though was the big downfall. You see it was already bad between Grandma Helen and mama but, man ever since the religion thing it had gotten worse. I told you guys that all of this started to tie in at some point.

The religion not only kept me questioned by many, but it pushed my parents away from people, and it pushed people even further away from us. Everybody in the hood knows that ever since the movie Friday came out starring Smokey talking about Jehovah's return in that first scene, that no one would like us now. I wasn't even a Jehovah Witness because I had never been baptized like my parents!

Helen started bashing my mother before me like she used to, but this time, it was worst. She talked badly about the religion so much that my mother stopped coming around her family as a whole. It wasn't until one night I'll never forget that sealed the deal. My mother got off work, picked me up from home, and headed to my grandma's house to have a serious one on one talk with her about their relationship. She wanted to talk to her about everything from her childhood all the way up to this point in their lives.

When we got there, my mother was torn down by the results. Questions started coming out like, "Why do you hate me? What did I do to you so wrong? Why did you hate my daddy so much? What can we do to resolve this please? The conversation didn't last a good hour guys!

To make matters worse, Mr. Eddie Lee from across the street was sitting in on the conversation as well – high as a kite too. He shouldn't have even been there if you ask me. He was said to be secretly having relations with my grandma at the time but that doesn't matter.

The point is, if I could change that day back I would because my mother cried her butt off from the time she started talking until the time we drove all the way back home, she was hurt. At that moment, I didn't know why she brought me, but right now today I'm glad she did. After I heard and saw the nasty way my grandma treated my mother for absolutely no reason, it wasn't until I had gotten older that I realized where my mistreatment came from.

At that time, I didn't understand though, which caused my life to turn into a world of change in the near future, and I started to hate my mother. I didn't speak to or see my grandma in years after that. I was getting ready to go to high school when my life changed drastically again. From here on, my story began to reopen chapters that I had buried like that of New Orleans. I hope the story has been interesting so far but it's about to become even more interesting!

CHAPTER 10

NEW FAMILY

"There's no other love like the love for a brother. There's no other love like the love from a brother."
- Astrid Alauda

After the disconnection happened between my mother and my grandma Helen, my mother decided to reconnect with my Aunt Janice. I think my Aunt Janice wanted to be back around anyways, to see if I had told my mother what they had told me about being adopted but I still hadn't said anything, even though it was bothering my life. Even though I tried to erase it, that day just kept popping up – of them telling me about my life. Now, my auntie also knew that I was probably, catching hell with my parents along with the rest of my family.

So, she decided to offer that I start coming around her more. "Now you know you need to start letting him around these boys more when they're not in school. These badass boys ain't nothing but his brothers. He needs somebody to hang around you know, and they miss him. Now, Linda you know how your dad was about family." Aunt Janice said as she sipped on her OE 40. My mother looks at me, rolls her eyes, and said, "No New Orleans trouble down here with them boys you hea!" I looked at her frowning but it suddenly turned into a smile as my cousins came running out of their trailer to me like I was famous! "What's up big bro?" Tray said to me catching his breath.

I just smiled at them, and we ran down the road together while my mother shouted out, "YOU CAN STAY HERE WITH THEM FOR A COUPLE OF DAYS!" Man was I excited to be with the baby G's. We suddenly stopped up the road and they looked at me as Tray would go on to say, "Say bro! You can't be leaving us like this no more cuz for real! We family and we brothers. Let's go hit that nigga Crazy Man up though for some food!" I looked at him, nodded my head, and followed them to another trailer.

By the way, I quickly found out that trailers were popular living homes in the country where we lived and people had no shame in how bad they looked. This was definitely the hood hands down. My cousins had moved from James Rd also into a very small town called Roseland. Their mother and father Darrel had finally separated and so did my Aunt Janice and Uncle Terry. The abuse I saw in person with both relationships was mind-blowing! Anyways, we finally make it to this guy named Crazy man's trailer, and he had a bus load of junk food.

It felt like the lady in New Orleans with the snacks and freeze pops in the hood or the ice cream man rolling in his van. We grabbed something with the change we had and walked back to the crib where my cousins lived. That night was one of many nights we would go hungry together with no food at all. Keisha would be out clubbing, Aunt Janice would be drunk, and we would be stuck looking crazy. So as a result, that left me in charge of everything since I was the oldest. One thing about that was, I knew how to survive.

I remember going hungry in the city for many of nights and also watching my father grill all the meat because our lights were cut off and he didn't want anything to spoil. "Ima take care of y'all I promise you!" I remember saying to my cousins as I would open up two cans of peas and spread it out between all six of us. No microwave and the stove had no gas! All I could think of was these dudes ain't no better than me! Just boyz in the hood like NWA or something. Now you may ask yourself where did six come from in eating those peas? You see it was only five of us boys, but there was a new addition to the clic.

My little cousin KeKe was born a couple of years back. She was the sister and the only girl to Tray, Dede, Bo, and Mun. So yes, I use to watch over her as well and she dealt with everything we dealt with. When we hit the bottle to get drunk, she did too. We broke all the rules in Roseland from stealing to starting fights and even fighting each other. We were family, and I will never forget those times and I damn sure won't forget what I'm about to tell you guys right now.

One weekend we all decided to ride our bikes a little further away from the trailer. I can't remember how but I had heard that one of my biggest crushes had just moved into Roseland not too long ago. "So they got this hot girl that I'm in love with named Robin Warford, you know her cuz?" I asked serious as a pitbull. "Man, you love her? Bro you tripping, but yaa she just moved around the corner! You want to see her?" Tray asked me as I froze up. I replied to him scared as hell saying, "Nah man, I'm good I just wanted to know!"

I promise you my cousin Tray had the evilest laugh saying to me, "Thissssss nigggggaaa scarrreeeddd man hahaha!" He sounded like Young Slim from the movie «The Wood.» I remember in my room after that beat down I took from my father and the things I'd dealt with, with my mother causing me to make an oath to myself that I would never be picked on, touched, or punked again. So, I quickly reversed my fear and said to my little cousins, "I bet I beat y'all to her location ya heard me!» In my New Orleans voice! I had said I loved her, but I didn't know what that meant at all.

Maybe it was her smile or her pretty light skin color that got my attention, I didn't know. So, Tray led the way laughing as we all jetted full speed miles away, turning into what seemed to be some apartments. Tray walked up to one of the doors and knocked on it. As he steps back, you can guess who opened the door quickly but comes out halfway slowly. "Hey y'all wassup?" Robin said as she glowed in the sun. I stood there frozen once again, scared as hell! Tray blurts out of nowhere, "Big cuz wanted to see you. He said y'all use to be friends when he was at Westside. It's messed up how people use to treat him. They don't know what he used to go through but WHAT I DO KNOW, is my man's got a crush on you hahaha!!"

I remember him saying those exact words like it was yesterday, as I started thinking to myself, «Wow, way to go with that introduction Tray!» "Hey Josh! I didn't even recognize you; you look different now. What's been up with you though?" She asked as we stood outside. We talked for like 30 minutes. I had remembered how she and I would run around the class together, and people use to ask us if we liked each other. She would just smile at them and say, «Josh is just my friend, that's all.»

In my heart, I felt like with all I had been going through, I was the last thing on hers or any girls list for that matter. All the popular guys wanted her as well, so I never bothered asking her out to be my young girlfriend. So, we said our goodbyes and that day would be the last time I'd ever see Robin Warford in person again. It was nightfall by the time we left, and we proceeded to ride in the streets like we were grown. Everybody in Rose Town knew who we were. The kids that would be underage drinking while watching boys shoot dice under the tree.

Watching some cats do drugs or shoot dice was all too familiar with us. We blended in as if we were grown. Witnessing someone getting beat with a bottle and then getting pissed on afterward was amazing to me over a game. I remember one night we all rode back to the trailer late and my arm was bothering me. Dede asked me what was wrong with my shoulder. I went on to tell them the story about the drive-by shooting, a bullet skipping my shoulder, and how this guy named Unc saved me numerous times like an angel. "It gets really sore sometimes but I'm aight.

Nobody in the family knows but y'all so keep it low." I told them as they nodded their heads and agreed. I could remember how the woman put bread on the wound, some medical stuff, wrapped it up, and I'd kept all this from my daddy nem! Amazing I thought.

Well moving forward, I was in the country sitting outside my parent's crib as I noticed next door, another trailer had been moved into that lot space and a raggedy burgundy colored van pulled up in front of it. A woman, a man, and five children hopped out of it and walked towards the trailer. "I guess they're the new neighbors." I thought to myself, as I couldn't help but notice one of the children out of the five. A short yellow kid with a curly fro and a loud country mouth yelling, "Touch me again and ima slap the taste out your mouth girl!"

The dark skinned man driving who had seemed to be the father looked back with a mean look saying loudly, "Trey, you better stop that s#$% before I put my foot in your ass boy!" "Man, daddy that's her shoots, tell Ashley something!" Trey replied. "Both of y'all stop it and I mean it!" He ended. Not even ten minutes later, the young boy introduced himself to me saying, "What's up man, you stay here? We just moved here the other day.

That's my daddy Leroy, my stepmother Caroline, my sisters Ashley and Goldie, and my stepsisters Keosha and Faylicia." "O ok cool. So let me guess, your name is Trey, right?" He nodded yes. "Well, I got a little cousin named Tray you should meet one day," I told him, as he agreed excitedly and proceeded to walk back to his trailer. Not long after that introduction, Trey became a friend to me, Raymond, and family to my parents. It wasn't long before I started labeling him as my brother despite my past.

At the time, my parents were becoming more and more spiritual, which caused me to have to participate in the religion more even though I wasn't baptized. They would bring my little brother Trey as well. My father also let him start working with us to make himself some extra money. Together, people started noticing how fast we worked and how good each job looked when we were finished. From working for the big time Simpson lawyers, to the Jewelry shop owners, even Mr. Biggs who sat in the Master Chef of Amite every morning eating breakfast with other big shots.

Well, as time passed, Trey too would witness my mother, the angry Linda Jackson. "Bro why she so mean man?" He asked, curiously. "Sometimes I will be like man she won't even let him out of the house or his room! I'm confused bro like it doesn't make no sense?" He continued as I sat next to him embarrassed. After a long silence, I remember telling him, "If you ready to hear it all I'll tell you but, you'll be the only person that knows about me besides the family, the baby G's, so keep it all between me and you ya heard me. "Ok big bro you have my word!" He said. There was a small store up the road that I, Trey, Ray, and Ryan used to walk to called B&V's. He walked beside me as I told him everything from my past up until then.

He was young, but he was understandable and he couldn't believe it. To my surprise in return though, young as he was at the time, he still had a story of his own. Trey didn't know his birth father just as I didn't as well. Mr. Leroy was just his stepfather that signed his birth certificate and took great care of him and his sisters. Of course, even before he told me, I knew his mother was white because he and his sisters were very light skinned. She lived in Florida at the time, and she never came to see her children anymore. He and Leroy would argue all the time, but he loved the only father that he knew to death.

If you guys pay close attention in the following chapters, you'll find Trey's story to become very and I mean very interesting! As we ended our stories off, we automatically grew closer to one another like family. "Ima always keep you on my side as my little brother till we die ya heard me! As for my mama, I can't stand her! I'm going to figure out a way to get away from both of them bro. When I do, I promise I ain't never coming back!" I informed him as he looked up at me laughing as if I were joking. "If there is a real God, he knows I'm serious!" I said.

With his country accent, he replied once more saying while laughing, "Aight nah bro, if you leave, don't leave me, but we're not walking by nobody trash at night hahaha!" He'd remember me telling him about me and Martin's encounter with a dead body. After our walking convo, that was just one of those memorable days that I remember that sets the tone on our road to being close brothers! One weekend, I met the rest of his family as well.

Now, it was ok to meet his aunties, uncles, and cousins like Essie, Jeremy, Curtis, his grandma, hotboy Ronald and April but, there was one that made my heart drop when I met here. Amanda beautiful yellow bone Davis Woohoo! She was gorgeous every time I saw her! Always with a little ponytail in the back of her head pointed to the side. She was a tomboy, a fighter, and just as loud-mouthed as Trey was. She and Robin were a lot similar! She was from Mississippi living with her grandmother at the time which was also where Trey used to live before he moved to the trailer park. So, they were very close with each other which put me right in the driver's seat to get at her.

The funny part was that I found out later on that she had a crush on me as well but she lived so far away. I said to myself when I get older, I'll get her with no problem. I remember seeing her for the last time at her grandmother's house in her room looking down at her as she looked up into my eyes. "Josh and Trey y'all come the hell on here nah we finna go," Leroy yelled as we ran out to the van. I had ridden with them to Mississippi just so I could see her that day but she didn't know that. As we drove off that night, she and her brother Jeremy stood in the doorway as she smiled continuously. That would also be the last time I saw her around this period as well. In the future, I had a great feeling I may see her again!

As I look out my window in the back seat accompanied by the family, I see nothing but miles and miles of beautiful land quickly passing my eyes as the vehicle continued to drive. This part of my story is a blur, but I do remember this scene in my head of all of us packed in the car like sardines. My aunt Janice was visiting someone in the penitentiary. All I know is that this particular person killed someone, and a second person we used to visit was beating up women. Now that right there; wasn't anything new in our family.

Damn, nearly everybody was getting beaten up. Even on my daddy's side of the family, My Aunt Neecee and her husband always fought, especially her baby daddy Willie! I made a young vow to myself that I would never beat a woman. Secondly, after all, I'd been through with the white folks back in New Orleans, I wasn't about to go to jail either. Hypothetically speaking, I was already in jail with my mother anyways and I started at an early age! So, I made up my naive mind that I wasn't going that route. I did take something positive from those rides, and that was the nature.

I focused on things that other kids did not as I said before in my story. The landscape and large amounts of land reminded me of my Grandma

Helen's place, which I missed so much. I would daydream, thinking of myself owning every bit of it one day. My mind would often go off into different places dreaming of traveling to different areas I learned about in school. I was amazed by the movement of the flowers swaying in the wind to the perfectly straight lines of farmland growing as long as my eyesight could reach.

Cows and horses would roam those lands as if it were their own. I just added it to the list of things I promised myself to get when I got older. Come to think of it; I tried to leave the house as much as I could. I would take trips with Leroy and Tray to the Manchac Swamp as well to go fishing at times. The two of them were pros but I mainly focused my eyes on the gators. Television shows these days such as 'Swamp People' was and is the real deal! You would always catch a gator being smart as ever in the deep end of the water, as I sat on the bank.

One minute the head is up in the deep end far away; then it disappears dropping under the water, then it pops up again a little closer, disappears again, then it wounds up even more closer. Of course, I don't have to tell you guys what happened next seeing that there was no next to that story because my ass was up and in the van as Trey and Leroy laughed like crazy! I was not going to be that thing's lunch! Now that I think about it, when I was growing up, there would always be rumors about the dead bodies being dumped in the Manchac from the killings in my hometown.

It makes sense now with all those gators! Good times no doubt they were with my boy and Leroy despite that though. Well, when my mother got into her mean 'forget the world spells,' it would be long periods of time before I got to spend time with the young family. She and her family were just so damn distant and hateful. It's so bad that even today, I don't know a lot of their names and they won't even speak to me if they see me.

Despite that, baby G's and I were close. It was that time for us to link back up and for them to meet Trey. It took a while for them to get along at first. I'd even break them up a couple of times from fighting each other – that is Trey and Tray. Eventually, they accepted him as part of the family though. Little brother Trey was the king at stealing and he had no heart behind what he did. This dude would even steal from his family members; he was that bad. They also loved how he did not back down from anybody and when we went hungry, he went hungry too. Time after time we would travel to Fluker, La because we had family out their deep. I would look amazed at the run down trailers, the clothes hanging on lines (which I use to wash by hand growing up in the bathtub), the children running around barefooted with their shirts off, the vehicles with big rims on them, and the men standing outside in front of certain houses.

I had been there and lived that with my father in New Orleans being born and raised around drugs. For the first time, that's when I noticed that trap houses were everywhere and that the hood was likewise. Country or not, we were some young niggas surrounded by the hood, and I just couldn't seem to escape it. This is who I was and my entire family on my mother's side. As I write this, I remember vividly the images that repeated in my head of my grandfather getting killed right in Fluker.

It was like a live video playing in my mind as if I were there. I had those type of visions a lot guys like that song from Houston that says, "My mind is playing tricks on me." Well, this would be one of those times! Picturing my mother hold her father in her arms while he bled to death as she screamed was a horrifying image. I couldn't imagine what my mother went through mentally after going through that! The question is, why were these images being played in my head, and how could I imagine these images so easily when I wasn't even born yet?

I never found the answer, but I knew it had something to do with my rare thinking. The crazy thing is that no one talked to me about this moment. I had to find these things out like this on my own by overhearing the conversations and chit chat. So, leaving out of Fluker we would just take Hwy 51 to get back to Roseland. Well, on the way back we used to stop at this small store across the tracks in Tangipahoa, La. This was also a small town we grew familiar with that was of course hood as well.

I remember a man walking up to my Auntie asking if she had something on her. We all looked puzzled as he lifted his finger to his nose sniffing it really hard, making a noise. That's exactly the way he asked her too, using that exact sound language! Although we were puzzled at first, we all finally looked at each other because we caught on to what he was asking for. He wanted cocaine, and he knew auntie kept it along with her husband Uncle Terry and their son Tone.

Actually, at the time, I believe Tone was in jail for drugs or either beating up his beautiful longtime girlfriend. You see, we knew all about them because we once walked in on my Auntie doing it off of a spoon with her lighter! Tray nem used to cry, but I didn't care at all because it was normal to me early on. Also, in front of that exact store, stood a lot of dudes every time we would come through as if they ran the place! I knew exactly what they were doing as well, but one of the things I saw one day sparked something in me.

This guy pulled up with a beautiful paint job on his car, huge rims, and a mouth full of golds like they wear in New Orleans! He gave each of us a $20 bill out of a big grip of cash he pulled out. "Y'all lil wodies don't need to be getting in no trouble hea!" He told us as he got back in his car while fixing his jewelry.

Without wasting any time Dede blurts out, "I'ma always get in trouble boy but that big clean son!" Before I knew it, Auntie Janice slapped him in the back of the head and told him to get in the car! She used her cold hand to slap him too, after dipping it in that ice for a cold beer so, you know it hurt hahaha!

As they all got in the car, I stood there still in amazement holding my $20 thinking to myself, "I'ma have all that and more one day for real!" Meanwhile, reality set back in, I was still poor, and it was time to head back to school. I skipped my Junior High career in the book because it was the same ole stuff but a tad bit different because I had classmates that would eventually become friends then family. Trey and I had become even closer and he was deeply accepted in the family now but the good things always seemed to go bad for me.

One day, my mother got a phone call saying that Tray of the baby G's, his sister, and his brothers were moving up north to like Oklahoma or something, with their mom for a change in their lives. The crazy part is that my mother seemed not to care. She told me that they needed to get away because of future trouble and their father's influence.

To me, my Uncle Darrel was a hard worker that had some of the same issues my father had so that was a lie! I was hurt for real and I even became affected by their decision to all leave. You see, that was my out away from home and without them, I was stuck back in lockup mode, besides working with my father.

On top of that, Trey's stepfather Leroy had been in an accident on a horse ride along with a list of bad health habits that would later cause him never to walk again! He would eventually be put in a wheelchair after his leg amputation. I felt the Martin and GG saga all over again saying to myself,

"Here we go again, and from what I heard, they're not coming back! I can't believe I'm going through this again!" Yes, I still had my little bro Trey but these situations would really start to affect me mentally. My thoughts became more in-depth about what the hell was going on with me.

I didn't even finish getting more about my adoption, even though I tried to leave it alone. Not to mention, I didn't even get to say goodbye or at least hear their voice on the phone one last time! The only family from my daddy's side that really felt like blood, treated me like a brother, and accepted me, was taken away from me. Man, I was getting older, smarter, and my mother was on my back even harder than before, and my father was a capital yes man behind her every move.

With this new religion, they were changing, but I was only becoming worse. Our views were different, my mother's anger got the best of her actions, school became different, the girls were feeling out, and my chapter was about to change in the prime of my teenage years kicking in! I was about to experience one of the biggest changes in my life that you all just have to know about... So, keep reading!!!

CHAPTER 11

FROM A BOY TO A MAN

"I learned that courage was not the absence of fear, but the triumph over it. The brave man is not he who does not feel afraid, but he who conquers that fear!"
- Nelson Mandela

It has been quite some time now since the baby G's left, but I would never forget my little brothers. As my time grew, I'd developed some new friends, though I did start to become a little confused about the consistency of people leaving me since I was a child. I still had my brother Trey and Raymond who taught me a lot about sports and he even helped me join the football team at school. Now playing ball was good because it taught me discipline in another form, believing in myself, and it created massive muscles on my body that made me have very high self-esteem.

It also gave me a distance away from my parents, especially my mother! The downfall of my career was the support. My parents probably came to a hand full of games, my mother always had a problem with me coming home late from practice, and I was still working with my father, so I would be very tired all the time. I would quickly become involved with another set of friends or shall I say the family that would change my life drastically! "Say what you need to do bruh, is start messing with us for real!" Charlie said to me slowly but seriously after practice one day.

I respond to him quickly telling him, "Yaa I feel you bro, I just been through a lot ya heard me. "Well, just know, you ain't never gotta worry about nothing, me and Craig got you fool," replied Charlie as he dapped me off and left. Now, you all remember earlier in my story where I met these two guys in class that were cousins, and one of them got his first tattoo in the fourth grade. Well, he is the one that I had the conversation with. Now throughout junior high, then high school, I began to develop a bond with Craig first, then finally Charlie the hard head. Craig and I became family as time went by, which meant that his entire family had become my family.

The funny part about the situation was that Treys step sisters Faylicia and Keosha were also a part of the family. You see their father was from the fox hole as well and he was also cousins to Craig and Charlie. It was weird to me, but it was perfect also because Trey would be staying out in the hole with them getting into all kinds of trouble. I say by the time I was around fourteen years old, I started staying with Craig or either Charlie.

Of course, it was never my mother that agreed on anything; it was always my father begging her to let me do something besides work, go to meetings, and come home. You see as I got older, I understood my mother wasn't as crazy as I thought she was. She knew what I did in New Orleans, the environment I was used to being around, and she felt that if she and my father were trying to change, I should too. As I told you all before, I didn't quite know what it was about me, but I just had a different thought process on life itself.

Secondly, I'd been held captive for too damn long, and I was done. It was time to go after whatever my mind was pushing me towards. In my heart, I had already started to feel like a man. I woke up one day and said to myself; it was time to stand on my own two feet or either let this pain continue. I looked at my father one evening, told him I was ready for a regular job and that I had wanted to quit working with him. It was fun drinking beer while looking at women and working with my father, but at an early age, it was time to move on.

I knew if I were to get a job, I would need to have a stable ride to get around. So, instead of your typical teenager looking for their parents to hook them up on a ride, I didn't allow it. My mother had an old green Dodge Neon with the ugly bubble lights sitting in front of the trailer, barely using it, so I asked, "O say mama?

Since I'm getting a job, ima need transportation, so let me make you a deal. What you say, if I use your car for about a month to stack two paychecks and, I pay you $800 for a car you barely use?" She answered quickly saying, "Ok, you can have it because the damn thing is just taking up space but, ima tell you this boy, I want my damn money, and I want help around here every month you heard me! You remember, ain't nothing free in this world I don't care if I am your mother!" "Yes ma'am I replied excitedly. Honestly, I didn't care if she was my mother or not! I'd learned from my father already how to stand on my own two feet and how to hustle.

My mother wasn't even a huge fan of graduating or college anyway because she didn't graduate. All she cared about was a job or getting money some kind of way. Quickly, I paid my mother for the car. I was fourteen years old with no license riding around everywhere at the bottom of Louisiana.

I would even take trips back home to New Orleans and Kenner from time to time looking at the few places I'd been. At this time in my life, I spent most of my time with my new friends and my little brother Trey. I'd slowly stirred myself away from Raymond. He and his family had just too much going on, from fist fights with his dad, jail, drugs, and the list goes on. That was still my boy don't get me wrong, but there was just a certain 'back at home vibe' I'd felt with the fox hole.

It was country surrounded by close family and trailers together. I would ride out there every chance I got. It opened my eyes to surrounding places that made our high school look like a small white campus that people thought was soft. So let me explain. Jewel M. Sumner High consists of, in my opinion, more white people than black.

When I was growing up all the way until I went to Westside, the schools I attended were flooded with black people. So, when people look at Sumner, they may think that there's no such thing as hood people involved, tough neighborhoods, or even drugs.

Maybe one may think from the outside looking in that because it wasn't a big school or it wasn't predominantly black, that there was no trouble to get into. Well, I must inform everyone up and down Interstate I-55 that this was not the case. The whites and blacks indulged in anything you can think of that you see going on in the hood. The area just didn't get any props because it was so small compared to your bigger cities. Secondly, there was no marching band or any history of sports championships.

Now, I told you earlier in the story that nobody messed with Charlie's place of stay, which was the fox hole. Well, there were other close-knit families that also had their own holes as well. You see in the city, we would call the seventh ward, Susan Park in Kenner, or Uptown, for example, the hood, whereas here in the country there would be family oriented holes.

The Mack hole was just flat out notorious anytime you have people with walkie talkies telling you who was coming in and out, back in the days. Silver Creek had several family members who were either in jail or out on papers likewise with the Mack hole.

The Fox hole which I will explain more in depth is under the hill which I can't forget about, Wilmer, and all the way to Franklinton, and the list goes on of small areas! This was all considered across the river or the ATR. The areas across the river were infested with drugs, convicted felons, and children that were cursed before they even knew how to read. These places also bred some of the most talented athletes of the school system.

This sort of reminded me of G and his family back in New Orleans. These families all shared the same type of mentality. Kansas Fox, better known to me as my Mama Boosie, was Craig's mother and also one of the most important people in my story. Until now, when she's reading this, she probably didn't even know it herself and what she has done for my life. Jazmine, Craig's sister also lived in the trailer with them along with a guy named Hugh Miller… He was in a relationship with Mama Boosie at the time, and despite it being weird to my young eyes, he still was cool with me.

I mean EVERY TIME I spent time at their trailer, Mama Boosie cooked a meal for Craig and me. Charlie stayed walking distance in the hole so he would walk over every time always too late saying as he laughed, "J, you and Craig always eating everything up before I get here, damn man!" "That's big boy is seating it all up! You know he ain't used to that!" Craig replied in a joking but truthful manner. You see, they all knew partially a little bit about where I'd come from. I never had hospitality like this in my life, besides being by my grandmother. I hadn't seen her in years following her and my mother's altercations either. "See big Jizzle, I told you we got you bruh; you know Boosie gone treat you like her own fool," Charlie said seriously this time.

It was so true about what he said that day, as Boosie would be at all of our games screaming for her son, Charlie, and me. She was amazing! I didn't get a chance to understand at the time until I'd gotten old enough to write this. Jizzle was the name they gave me followed by a B that stood for baby... I was from New Orleans so they'd taken the name from the rap artist BG, turned it backwards and pronounced a J instead of a G.

It was like routine afterward for Charlie and I to get in the truck with Hugh Miller, head to the store for some Seagram's gin, and a couple of bottles of OE. I'm convinced that as I write this, no one from the beginning of my story until now, cared about alcohol consumption or drugs before the age of twenty-one!

My boy Craig didn't indulge in any of the drinking or crazy stuff we did, and he mostly kept a level head. Craig had dreams and it showed every time he stepped on the football field. The Fox boys were some of the best ballplayers in the parish even though Charlie was the bad boy; he was just as talented as Craig. They had a major influence on me on and off the playing field. You see while playing ball with my boys; I was still participating in the Kingdom Hall activities due to my parents.

On Tuesday nights, there were ten-minute sections called 'the school' where the young boys in the Hall were given a chance to read certain scriptures out of the Bible that we were asked to look over a week in advance. All my mother seemed to care about was my participation in the religion some kind of way. I'd remember the nights she would beat my hands for better gestures and reading skills like that of a slave which I would implement in every reading I did... I wasn't the typical reader either.

I could look at the crowd in front of me and memorize the scriptures without taking my eyes off the crowd but a split second at a time. To be honest, she was wrong but she had turned me into a young Malcolm X or Martin Luther the way I could speak to crowds without fear. This period of my life only lasted for a short time though. I had become close friends with Tuti, Nick, Trell, and a few more cats out of the hood that were all sports players.

We were all approached each at separate times by an elder of the hall saying to us, "Now I understand you play a few sports at your school at the time. Well, coming from the Bible's point of view we can no longer allow you and any of the other young guys to continue in the school at this time until you let the sports go entirely, says Jehovah God."

Of course, my mother already wanted me to quit sports, but now she did more than ever. I wasn't about to quit anything, and neither did the other guys. I'd learned so much from my coach, after all, I'd been through up until this point in my life so; I wasn't about to leave my team. Secondly, I was still too young to hear something like that from an elder, telling me it was Jehovah's choice along with everything else I'd dealt with due to this religion.

I'd told myself from that day forward that I respect it for changing my father entirely, but I was still personally done. Meanwhile, my mother was still smoking her weed, while cursing at me every chance she got because of what everyone else was doing to her!

My father, although a changed man, still had his women he introduced me to behind my mother's back that he did yard work for. A heavy player he continued to be, but I never told my father I'd gotten fed up with that life as well. You see, when my mother took those trips looking for her brother Michael on several occasions, I will study every piece of the situation.

Michael was the brother in the family that also had a tough relationship with my grandmother, causing him to leave home early and live on the streets. My mother was his comfort source like a second mother he was close with. So, when he called to give her a location of his whereabouts, she'll come running making my father drive. Sometimes, he wouldn't even show up and would later call her saying never mind. Those events would crush my mother, seeing her little brother on his on out in the streets for so long going from state to state.

Little did my parents know, was that I'd gotten so smart that I'd studied that for myself, to be on my own soon. I knew that I would have to think like a man if I did that. I'd been exposed to homelessness so; I knew I could even live in my car. Since the school wouldn't allow me to park without a license and a tag from the school, I would ride with Michael Easley every day.

That was another partner I played ball with and secondly, his father owned a chain of convenience stores we would go to for all of our alcohol, so he was well off. Keep him in mind as I go deeper into this chapter.

The influence that the Fox boys placed on me had become a part of who I was, especially with football. I started taking it seriously, which caused different schools, the coaches, and even the players' parents to take notice of me. There was one lady, in particular, that would scream to the top of her lungs at every game for her son and me. I'd felt special how she would come up to me after the games, letting us know our good hits and all of our stats.

Now, one of the things my teammates use to do for great chemistry is meet up after every Thursday practice, by one of the parents' house to eat and chat about the game the next night.

I never attended once and this lady was getting fed up with asking me eagerly, "Now JJ, are you going to come to our home 2mrw and eat up some stuff or what? I've never seen you come and you need to be with us while we get pumped up for the game on Friday. "Yes ma'am, I'll be there

I promise you!" I replied confidently. In the back of my mind, I knew I had answered too quick, but, I was tired of being left out of everything. I wanted to be a normal kid that didn't always work, clean the house, and sit in a room with no television doing pushups all night!

So, when I made it home, I dapped my boy Mike off and ran into the house and immediately asked my mother, "Can I go to the teammates gathering tomorrow? I've never been and they asked me could I finally come before the big game on Friday." My mother sat there at her computer puffing her cigarette for five minutes before she looked at me and said, "No, you cannot, but what you can do is clean up this house! You should be tired of playing that damn ball. You don't go to the Hall on Tuesday anymore because of that shit!

Now, tackle that damn room and one more thing, where is my $100 for this month?" I stared at her with a glaze in my eye fed up! Quickly I replied saying, "Where all my money from my bank account I've been saving up first of all? You ain't gonna do nothing but go to the Truck Stop with this $100 and gamble it away!" After I had given her the money, I walked away quickly to the back room mumbling under my breath, "I'm tired of this shit for real!" "Boy, who do you think you're talking to in my house?" She asked. I politely looked up and told her, "You, why wassup?"

That night, was the last piece of crap I was going to take. When I looked her in her eyes, I had sensed fear in her. She knew the person she called her son was boiling. So, she said nothing more, walking out of the room while calling my father to the top of her lungs! He wasn't even at home. I didn't hear from him or my mother again for the rest of that night. The following day after practice, I rode with Mike and the rest of the teammates to the lady's home. When I sat in her beautiful home surrounded by the most white people in my entire life, I felt so good. I had forgotten all about what I was going through and to top it off, the house was amazing.

It was a big beautiful brick home full of space and lots of land around it. Just what I had envisioned myself having in the future while riding to the penitentiary with my Aunt Janice. This was a different environment from hanging around in the hood and I placed this moment in my book because it meant a lot to me mentally.

Of course, later that night, I said my goodbyes to Mike as he dropped me off, and I go into the trailer, fully prepared for any consequences I would receive. By the time I had sat on the bed, I heard my father's footsteps slowly walking towards the room. "Son, lately, this house hasn't felt like a home in a long time.

You come into the house; you rarely say anything to us and, you don't even clean anymore like you're supposed to. You're always gone, and God also showed me a few things in your closet that will not be done in this house! Lastly, your mother told you that you couldn't go tonight with your team and you disobeyed her. Since you think you don't have to abide by these rules around here, you can get out of this house."

With everything in me, I wanted to respond to my father by asking him, "Why are you just now coming into my life trying to make rules after being in the streets? Why haven't you asked me what's wrong or what I've been through with your life growing up? Why have I been cleaning and working since I was five years old? Why did I grow up around women you slept with, drug houses, and crackheads? Have you asked your God Jehovah why I don't talk to you all?

Lastly, even though there is more, why the hell you kicking the little boy out that saved your life multiple times and who was never told he was adopted?

"No, No, No, I can't respond with that it's too much at this time!" I told myself quickly. So, I looked up at my father with a smile on my face, and I politely said, "Ok, that's fine, see you guys one day." He looked back at me in a very shocking way as he proceeded to walk out.

By the time my father was comfortable in his room on the other side of the trailer, I was gone with Mike in the wind. I know you guys are probably asking how the heck I moved that fast. I was smart as I told you before. So, I had already got permission from mama Boosie to stay on her couch as long as I wanted to. As for the Fox boys, I told them way back that someday, I was leaving. Of course, I told Mike that night to be looking out for me. So yaa, all my bases were covered!

I finally made it to the Fox hole, I was greeted by mama Boosie letting me in, and straight to the couch I went to lay out. I laid there staring at the ceiling thinking about so much I'd been through from the time I could comprehend, up until this moment. The tears wouldn't fall, but I felt the pain as it kept me awake that night. The next night we had an important game that we won by our defense shutting the opponent out. I remember every time I made a big hit; I would look up at Boosie as she smiled at me but, no sign of my parents.

Despite what I had been through, I had the best time of my life away from home, laying my head wherever I could. I was living in the streets people! I was only fifteen years old on my own thanks to the love shown from Boosie and the Fox boys. I would eventually go on to tell everybody that I was adopted and a little bit about my upbringing. Everyone was shocked to hear samples I expressed! Months had passed and I still hadn't talked to my parents. Life is good right now, and as a matter of fact, I felt free!

As I went to my brother Treys trailer one night to talk to him about some things such as me leaving, I noticed a small car in the front loaded down with bags. I stood there and watched as my brother and his two sisters put all of their belongings into the vehicle. Suddenly, I saw a white lady talking to them, telling them to hurry as they got into the vehicle. It was their mother Stacy taking them away. My heart felt as if it had stopped. I had heard a while back that since Leroy had health and marriage issues that Stacy would come get them but, I didn't believe it.

The car slowly passed by as I threw up our brotherly sign and he threw up his. My partner, my best friend, my little brother, whom I had taught so much, was gone. Take a look at the early chapters of my story if none of you caught how many people had left me by now. So for me, this meant from this day forward my heart didn't need friends. Even if I had some, I would always prepare for the worst. I was a man at such a young age, and honestly, this was the time I needed to be told I love you the most, be held by a mother for the first time in my life, but that day would never come.

That whole new image I tried after the judge told me to get my act together before I moved to Amite, all the crying because of years of mental and physical beat downs, and all of my dreams and wishes for a better life was no more. I developed this defensive mindset and a "don't care" attitude. At this time, I was still living wherever I laid my head. A little off subject for a minute but I often question today's men that call themselves street or that came from nothing.

I feel like we all can voice our opinion and not say that my life at this time was harder than everyone or they don't have their own story, but I feel the shakes when I write. I was literally 15 years old sleeping from house to house or on park benches where I knew many people didn't come, homeless like once before. I was grazed by a bullet in my shoulder at too young of an age. I knew what crack cocaine, weed, and other hard drugs were before I knew I was adopted or how to read.

I was an alcoholic damn near. I started working, getting myself ready for school, and living a serious lifestyle by the age of 5. I was in court at the same time as my father, and I was a baby G by the age of 12 and 13. I was doing way too much at that age with my little cousins. I've been picked on, beat up, embarrassed. Some of my own family members treated me like dirt. I've been told by teachers I was terrible to be around and turn right around to be told by my mother that I could go right back where I came from. I saw dead bodies before I could even understand that subject.

My list up to this point in my story at 15 years old goes on with even more to come! My opinion as a studier of our world today is that so many people have a mother and they CHOOSE to go down a dark path. Even if one is raised by his grandmother or doesn't have his father, you still have someone to be there for you, understand you, and often allow you to know how important family is. I never even once had that in my life, until I met other families like the Foxes and the Fosters.

The first loving mother figure I had was Mama Boosie. At some point in my life, I started to envy those who had a family. It's no matter if you all fuss and fight! You have each other, and that's something I know I yearned for growing up. To call yourselves street niggas when you've had your mother to give you a place to stay, eat even if it was ramen noodles and say, "That's my baby!" Your grandmother signed for you that trap car and used her home to bail you out of jail. Yes you can still be street, but this book has shown everyone, I didn't have any of that.

Good as my father was raised, great of a heart he had, hard of a worker he was, and as spiritual he'd become, he still had no idea his son needed him. He and my mother were draining the life from me. This writing allows me to vent. So, to tie this in with my chapter, I had to be a different type of animal and a special young man. I already felt like an outsider but at this point in my life, I felt as if I was out of this world. From this moment on, it'll take a lot for me to get emotional again, cry, or be moved by anything. I'm trying to do the best to paint that picture for my readers on what I was going through at this time and how today society, in my opinion, is, spoiled. I would like to share more but we must move on.

On a Saturday evening C. Fox, SB, DJ and I were riding around when I got a phone call from Mama Boosie saying eagerly, "Son! I need you to get to my house. I have something to talk to you about ok." I immediately came to her crib to see what she wanted. "Hey, you know your mother called me," she said in a puzzled manner. I replied stuck and shocked, asking, "How the hell did she get your number? What did she say? Did she act stupid with you?" "Calm down boy and just listen! I don't know how your mama got my number at all. Yes, she tried to get crazy at first. She even asked me how could I take in a child that isn't mine. That's when I knew your mother had some issues because my heart is different.

We talked for quite some time, and I know you're not going to like this, but that is still your mother by law. Secondly, you are still a teenager that is not eighteen so; she has authority over you. Now, I know you don't want to hear any of this, but I want you to call her.

Can you do it for me and give her a second chance?" She asked after explaining what happened. I stood there with my heart in my stomach, thinking to myself, "Why me?" "Aight ima call her ya heard me, but if she acts stupid, I'm done," I replied. She smiled at me but finished by telling me, "Josh. I want you to at least finish school and graduate. You've been out here wilding as well, and I don't see you much anymore so, from now on, at least let me know where you are or where you're going ok," she said as she hugged me and walked back inside.

I took a long walk down the rock road pacing back and forth before I called my mother and then finally it happened. "Hello... Hello... HELLO!" My mother said three times before I say a word. "Wassam, you had wanted to talk to me?" So basically I'm going to explain how the conversation went. She started off by explaining that she had nothing to do with my father putting me out, which I told her that I felt it was a lie. She told me that she didn't want me to end up like her brother Michael and that some people we used to know back in the city children got murdered.

I wanted to ask her so badly, "What about the times you put me out and made me sleep outside in the rain while my father didn't come home?" Still that day, I didn't ask a word. Since I was so quiet on the phone, she went on to become forceful and frustrated. She started to demand I come back home or someone would be in trouble. So the truth is, it wasn't because Boosie told me to go back home but it was because I didn't want anyone to have problems because of me.

So, I agreed with her that I would come home. I didn't show up until about a month later, though. When I went back home, it wasn't long before it had gotten worse. I didn't care about school and at one time I was going to drop out. I told myself I was going to make myself finish because my mother didn't.

When I failed the Louisiana Leap test the first time, C. Fox and I were placed in the retest classroom with two of the finest girls in Sumner. Squilla and Shaniel Mack with a mouth full of gold out of the gangsta Mack Hole. Squilla was smart, so she helped me pass the second time! I would go on to graduate High School despite the negative things my mother said about school.

Afterward, I got a job at McDonalds but I was still in the streets. I was always working and when I was off, I was never at home. I even went to Southwest Mississippi Community College for half of a semester but it just wasn't for me. I turned down schools that wanted me to play ball because I had no love for it anymore. C. Fox didn't play anymore either, but Craig went on to play college ball.

It wasn't long before my father talked to me again about being on my own, but this time he did in a way that I knew was right and it really was time for me to move on. My relationship with my mother was just never there. I handled my business like a grown-up though and got my place. I was in the house with two old school vehicles; all the new Jordans stacked in my closet to the ceiling, porno flicks, drugs, alcohol, stacks of money, etc. I was untamed and still a teenager.

I was still back and forth from the hole to amite, and New Orleans. My bond with C. Fox grew stronger as time moved on. It began to be another chapter developing in my near future that would invite new people into my story, powerful situations, and a well calculated Joshua Jackson becoming smarter by the day. It's time for me to introduce the reader to a heck of a movie, so stay tuned!

(END OF PART 1 EBOOK SERIES)

SNEAK PEAK

I AM KING PART 2

This particular night after I left her crib, I decided to pull up on the side of the road in this pretty nice looking neighborhood at about 3 am, to get one of my guns out of the trunk. As I shut my hood, I jumped back into my car and as I started the car again. As soon as I pulled off, I noticed two police cars in my rear view both turning their flashing lights on. «Damn! Here we go man!»

I thought, as I quickly controlled my steering wheel with my left leg while I placed my gun in my glove box and my magazine in my console. Now, this neighborhood was dark, so I wasn't about to stop my car until I made it to a place full of lights or a gas station.

Finally, I found a light pole with bright lights and I stopped. «Aight, gun separated and in the right place, umm no more hot guns in my trunk, no dope on me, no pills, no alcohol, ok fasho I'm good.» I thought to myself carefully. I also questioned, «Why the hell are there two police cars though?» I'd been used to being pulled over of course for speeding, but this time was different.

As I was staring in my rearview mirror, I noticed that the first police; an old white man, just stood outside of his car and the second man was dressed in like those army cargo pants, which I thought was weird. As he walked up to my car, every bit of me wanted to put my gun back together and shoot at both of them. My mental calmness was so gone and secondly the way they stopped me was weird, so I wanted to protect myself but, it was too late.

«Joshua Jackson, what are you doing around here boy, this isn't your neighborhood is it and why didn't you stop immediately?» Asked the officer with army pants on. First of all, this long-faced big eared white man knew my name and secondly how can he tell me where I live? «No, this is not my neighborhood, I just like to ride through the night to collect my thoughts and mind my business. It was too dark back there so I pulled ahead to a lighted area.

May I ask how you know my name and why you are stopping me?» I asked as he stood there with a look of amazement at how I responded to him because I didn't give a damn! Meanwhile, the other officer was walking back and forth around my challenger, writing the whole time in a notepad weirdly. «You got any drugs on you or in your car Jackson?» He asked with a devilish glare in his eyes.

«Why would you think I have any drugs and why did y'all stop me!?» I asked getting aggravated now. Well, I guess he got tired of my smart mouth because he immediately told me to step out of the car and put my hands behind my back. If I would have known what I know now, I would have called someone when I got pulled over and videoed this illegal act also.

Not to mention, yea I was under some light but, nobody was around at all. Well check this out. As I put my hands behind my back, the older officer cuffed me against the hood while the army guy searched my car. «This is messed all the way up!» I thought while watching him pick up my gun. As I mentioned before, I was a heavy reader so I knew a few things about the law.

«Man, it's registered and it's separated just like the Louisiana law states.» I said. He looked at me with a grin and responded, «O yaa, well state this sense you think you're so smart mother******!» Immediately after his disrespectful words, he threw my gun in the woods! «I know you dealing drugs and when I catch your black ass, Ima throw you away. You think you can ride around like this and not be touched?» He rambled as it went through one of my ears and out the other one.

"Black Ass?" I thought. At this point I was in full «Ima kill his ass» mode. I was staring him down like a lion and breathing heavily with full tunnel vision. What happened next screwed me up instantly. The other officer came back from his car after running my name in the system thoroughly I guess and found nothing on me. As he walked up he said, "Hey Chad! Let him go. I'll keep an eye on him trust me.»

My heart must've dropped instantly! There was only one Chad I knew and everybody else, Chad Federal Agent Scott! I had just been harassed by the «Boogie Man» Chad Scott who got away with harassing everybody. He was the exact identical of the officers in the "Central Park 5" incident back in the 90s. Just imagine so many innocent people locked up behind his doings!

As they took the handcuffs off me, they pulled off slowly as I stood there still with a serious adrenaline rush. «I can't believe this! Out of all people they harass me. Dirty ass policemen!» Truth be told, the officer that was with Chad messed with me every chance he got! I wasn't the kind to tell or report something ever since I was a child so I just suffered the consequences of being black with a nice car and a pocket full of money so, I just dealt with it.

So that night, I fixed my car back nicely and finally, I drove off. As I drove home that night, all I could think about was all the sick things I heard about Scott and how he had damn near everybody spooked. He caused some of the toughest hustlers I knew, snitch on their own family members. He robbed people for their drugs and money and even set people up to get killed.

After my Uncle told me that story about him years ago, I knew he was raw. Needless to say, that would be the last time I ever laid eyes on Chad again. Now I heard more stories about him and a few people working for him that I clearly stayed away from but, no more seeing him around. Fast forwarding time as of right now, my cousin Courtney told me Chad was locked up but, I didn't believe it so I looked it up.

Sure enough, in the headlines it read that he had 11 counts against him and that 7 counts consist of charges including perjury, obstruction of justice and falsification of government forms. He is now on his second trial because of the jury being unable to reach a unanimous verdict on any of the seven counts. When I read it, I immediately jumped up with joy screaming, "HAAA!! Who's the black ass Muthaf*** now Scott HAHAHA!!!!!

You know the sad part about it though? He may not receive any consequences besides a slap on the wrist. Anyone that has come across me wanting to know why I feel the way I feel about police officers, this is why. I'm not saying I'm right about the way I feel, I'm just saying this and other events I went through caused my feelings.

I am KING Part 2 Coming Soon!

Order online at amazon.com and all other online distributors
Contact information:
joshuajackson15533@yahoo.com

Interested in Writing and or Publishing a BOOK???

Visit: www.A2ZBooksPublishing.net

www.ingramcontent.com/pod-product-compliance
Lightning Source LLC
Chambersburg PA
CBHW052142110526
44591CB00012B/1829